P9-CKP-830

WILLIAM BREWSTER
OF THE
MAYFLOWER

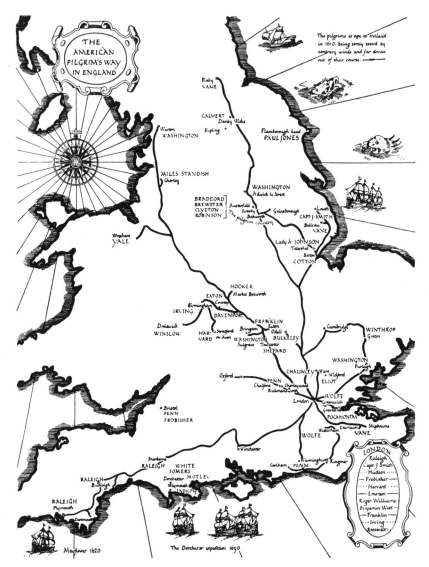

Babworth and the Pilgrim Fathers

WILLIAM BREWSTER
OF THE
MAYFLOWER

Portrait of a Pilgrim

by

DOROTHY BREWSTER

NEW YORK UNIVERSITY PRESS

New York 1970

To my friends Dr. Gulielma F. Alsop and
Fred Lawrence Guiles.

Copyright © 1970 by New York University
Library of Congress Catalogue Card Number: 73-133014
ISBN: 0-8147-0963-X
Manufactured in the United States of America

Foreword

Governor Bradford in the opening pages of his history, *Of Plymouth Plantation*, notes how Satan, "ever since the breaking-out of the light of the Gospel in England," maintained various wars against the Saints, in various ways, often by sowing errors, heresies, discords, and schisms among the Saints themselves. In Bradford's day, the errors and heresies were mainly theological. In our day, three hundred years later, Satan is as busy as ever, having added political, economic, and technological weapons to his arsenal, to promote dissension and stimulate persecution. During the recent McCarthy era in the United States, dissident saints and sinners alike were the objects of witch hunts—the popular word for the efforts of the Establishment to save the country from "communism"—an all-embracing danger. Many university teachers shared the honor of government harassment along with representatives of almost every section of society. It was when one of the Congressional committees got around to me and I was required to answer questions about my subversive activities, that I became curious about my ancestor, Elder William Brewster. What had he done, besides helping to found one of the most famous colonies of the New World, and in what precisely had he believed, to send him into exile?

Colonial Dames and Mayflower Descendants, justifiably proud of their ancestors, may think it odd that I had lived most of my life satisfied with what I was taught in school about the Pilgrims and the Puritans. Although my father and my grandfather were both William Brewsters, and I was told that I was a direct descendant in the ninth generation of Elder William Brewster through his son Jonathan, it never occurred to me to find out more about him than that he came to the New World with others, seeking freedom to worship God in their own way, landing as the waves dashed high on that "stern and rock-bound coast," inaccurately described by Mrs. Felicia Hemans in her famous poem, *The Landing of the Pilgrims*. The Puritans, who were seldom distinguished from the Pilgrims, were unpopular in the twenties, when I was in the early days of my university teaching. Among well-known writers who were then very much distressed about the low cultural level of our society, Puritans were regarded as mainly responsible for many of its ills—intolerance, narrow-mindedness, hostility to art and the joy of life. Those old Puritans believed in witches. They lived in the world of *The Scarlet Letter*. Freud was then helping to emancipate us from Puritanism.

During the years between the two World Wars, there were causes, some now half-forgotten, that kept concerned citizens (as we now call dissidents when we are being polite) busy agitating to correct evils and injustices, and to reassert traditional American freedoms in new situations, unknown to the Founding Fathers, and to realize the ever elusive American Dream. One of these causes, the Sacco-Vanzetti case, held the stage for years, becoming an international *cause célèbre*, and influenced the worlds of labor and law and politics and literature. Now and then those who persisted in active dissent dipped into early American history to find support for their arguments, and the Pilgrims were not forgotten. Scholars meanwhile were quietly busy delving into the past, seeking to clear the record of errors and myths. As we moved on through the Depression, the New Deal, the Spanish Civil War, and finally the Second World War, many members of the academic world, where I was living my professional life, became increasingly preoccupied with extracurricular activities: protesting, petitioning, boycotting, making speeches, forming committees, writing and supporting plays of social significance, marching in May Day parades, attending dinners to welcome freedom fighters and exiles from abroad and to raise money, picketing embassies, staging huge public meetings, forming United Front organizations with other sections of the community—doctors, scientists, lawyers, publishers, actors, left-wing labor leaders—all lumped together in current usage as Communists and fellow-travellers.

There was opposition to all these activities, in some places, but relatively few penalties at first to discourage the more respectable dissidents. Some books they wrote were banned in suburban libraries; some lecturers were barred from college campuses; some nice ladies belonging to the League of Women Shoppers were plucked off a picket line during a strike and sent briefly to jail. Radical weeklies rose and flourished, died or changed their names, and sometimes even survived. And history kept on presenting new disturbing challenges to action. It was not realized during those years, before Senator Joseph McCarthy took over the task of saving the country, that records were being kept and lists compiled, not only by law-enforcing agencies of all kinds but by volunteer groups of citizens alert to the "communist conspiracy." Anyone who got into the news by signing a petition, for example, or by protesting a Book Club selection of an anti-Soviet novel, after the Soviet Union had become an ally against Hitler, might find himself confronted in the press by a list of all the organizations, now labelled subversive, that he had ever belonged to. These lists, eventually sanctified by the Attorney-General, led to some law suits by a proscribed organization or two. Even if the suit were won in the courts and the organization cleared, its name remained tucked away in some government or committee file; and the legal costs spelled virtual bankruptcy. As late as 1969 names on these lists had a way of turning up to threaten the reputation or even the career of some civil servant or scientist or college professor. A well-known *New York Times* associate editor, Tom Wicker, in an article in *Harper's Magazine* for November 1969, "The Undeclared Witch-Hunt," writes of "the mounting stacks of personal dossiers in the government's secret chambers, with their unchecked and often ridiculous information." Spies and informers have been plentiful, as we shall see they were in Elder Brewster's day in England. But there were then no swift communication systems and no wire-taps and no concealed bugging devices. Had these technological aids been available to King James's pursuing officers, William Brewster might never have reached Plymouth, Massachusetts.

In 1952 and 1953 it became the turn of many educators in my part of the country to be summoned to Washington and questioned by one of several Congressional committees. In a closed hearing I was asked about my associations over the years, my political opinions and activities, my membership in organizations and on committees, my attendance at meetings, and my writings—all under oath with the threat of a charge of perjury always hanging over me if some informer produced a forged membership card, or something like that. I was finally dismissed. It was a minor affair, not the catastrophe such hearings were to many in the academic world. I was warned, however, that "they" knew where to find me, if they wanted me again. Times have changed: "they" did not know where to find Elder Brewster, of whose troubles I had been reminded during these proceedings. I happened to have a valid passport, and before "they" had time to follow me up and take it away, I went to England and Holland and did some research on my ancestor. But after 1953, and until 1957, I, like many others, had annoying passport difficulties. As I learned more about Elder Brewster's pre-Mayflower adventures, I began to feel a kind of long-range identity with him. Hadn't we both taught English to university students, joined with other like-minded people in discussing heretical ideas and promoting them in ways appropriate in his day and in mine? Hadn't we been summoned to account for activities considered subversive by government authorities, and were we not judged too dangerous to be allowed to leave the country? His adventures were of course incomparably more interesting than mine, but there is a significant resemblance between what happened to dissenters in the seventeenth century in England, and what continues to happen to them in the United States in the twentieth century. Not only is his story worth retelling in a coherent narrative, rescued from scattered sources, but it has contemporary relevance.

A Note on Sources

Pilgrim history really began in 1856 when Governor Bradford's manuscript, OF PLYMOUTH PLANTATION, was published in Boston. George F. Willison, in his introduction to the Classics Club edition (1948), tells the fantastic story of the adventures of the manuscript. Before that date Pilgrim history had been largely legend and myth. The Reverend Joseph Hunter, a fellow of the Society of Antiquarians in London and of the Massachusetts Historical Society, published in London in 1849 COLLECTIONS CONCERNING THE EARLY HISTORY OF THE FOUNDERS OF NEW PLYMOUTH; and in 1854 COLLECTIONS CONCERNING THE CHURCH OR CONGREGATION OF PROTESTANT SEPARATISTS FORMED AT SCROOBY. With these books William Brewster and the group that met at his home in Scrooby, Nottinghamshire, England, came into the picture. Another clergyman, the Reverend W. H. Bartlett, relying on what had become known of Bradford's manuscript—passages having been copied into church records and by early New England chroniclers—and on what Hunter had published, wrote THE PILGRIM FATHERS (1853, 2nd ed. London, 1854) with the subtitle OR THE FOUNDERS OF NEW ENGLAND IN THE REIGN OF JAMES THE FIRST. He describes Scrooby and gives some facts about William Brewster.

A promising clue in a book on the Episcopal Church in America (London, 1844) was followed up by still another clergyman, John S. Barry, who read a borrowed copy in 1855. As a result the manuscript was located in the library of Fulham Palace, one of the seats of the Bishops of London. How it got there has never been explained; and it was not until 1896, after much legal and diplomatic activity, that it came to rest in the State House in Boston. The Bishop of London, however, had allowed a transcript to be made, and that is how it came to be published in 1856.

The following year the first and only full length biography of William Brewster was published by Ashbel Steele: CHIEF OF THE PILGRIMS, OR THE LIFE AND TIME OF WILLIAM BREWSTER (Philadelphia, 1857). Steele's book is interesting, but to say the least is out of date, and very sketchy concerning Brewster's life in England and Holland.

After that we skip forty years, to 1897. George F. Willison, author of the invaluable SAINTS AND STRANGERS (1945), credits four great Pilgrim scholars for the

results of research during years of "exhaustive digging
in musty archives." They are:

Edward Arber, THE STORY OF THE PILGRIM FATHERS
    1606–1623 (London, 1897).
Henry Martyn Dexter and Morton Dexter, THE ENG-
    LAND AND HOLLAND OF THE PILGRIMS (Boston, 1905).
Charles Edward Banks, THE ENGLISH ANCESTRY AND
    HOMES OF THE PILGRIM FATHERS, WHO CAME TO PLY-
    MOUTH ON THE MAYFLOWER IN 1620, THE FORTUNE
    IN 1621, AND THE ANNE AND THE LITTLE JAMES IN
    1623 (Grafton Press, New York, 1929).

There is much information about Brewster in Walter H. Burgess's biography of John Robinson, the
pastor of the Pilgrim Fathers, published in London and
New York in 1920. Burgess relies upon the Dexters for
the Leyden period. Though we have only a few scattered facts about Brewster's years at Cambridge as a
student at Peterhouse, the background of student life
there is fully depicted in the study by William Pierce
of Brewster's classmate: JOHN PENRY, HIS LIFE AND
TIMES AND WRITINGS (London, 1923).

In all these books, in special studies of the Pilgrim
Press, and in other books and articles, there are numer-
ous references to Brewster in connection with other
persons and events. His name is prominent in indexes.
One must go through many books to collect the
disjecta membra of a life that was full of hazards, turns
of fortune and significant achievements.

Acknowledgments

In writing this book I have been encouraged and helped by my friends. Professor Ernest Griffin of York University, Toronto, and Mrs. Griffin toured the Scrooby neighborhood with me, and took pictures, some of which are reproduced in this book. Franklin Brewster Folsom, a *Mayflower* descendant, brought to my attention the researches of Mrs. Perle Lee Holloway into the ancestry of Elder Brewster's wife, Mary Wentworth. Mrs. Morris D. Brewster of Wilmington, Delaware, also a *Mayflower* descendant, and the wife of my cousin Morris Brewster, descended from Elder Brewster, has explored present-day Plymouth, Mass., and given me up-to-date information.

To the Reverend Edmund F. Jessup, Rector of Babworth, Nottinghamshire, I am indebted for permission to quote from his book, *The Mayflower Story*.

Contents

I

A Pilgrim

Under the date 1643 Governor William Bradford in his narrative, *Of Plymouth Plantation*, writes: "I must open this year with an event which brought great sadness and mourning to them all. About the 18th of April, died their reverend elder, my dear and loving friend, Mr. William Brewster, a man who had done and suffered much for the Lord Jesus and the gospel's sake, and had borne his part in weal or woe with this poor persecuted church for over thirty-five years in England, Holland, and this wilderness, and had done the Lord and them faithful service in his calling. Notwithstanding the many troubles and sorrows he passed through, the Lord upheld him to a great age; he was nearly fourscore years, if not quite, when he died. He had this blessing added by the Lord to all the rest; he died in his bed in peace, in the midst of his friends, who mourned and wept over him, and gave him what help and comfort they could; and he, too, comforted them whilst he could. His illness was not long, and until the last day he did not keep his bed. His speech continued until about the last half day and then failed him; and at about nine or ten o'clock that evening he died, without any pangs at all. A few hours before, he drew his breath short, and some few minutes from the end he drew it long, as a man fallen into a sound sleep—without any gaspings—and so, sweetly departed this life into a better."

The year according to our reckoning was 1644, and the date of his death therefore "about" April 18th, 1644. Bradford then says "something" of his life. He had spent "some little time" at Cambridge; attained some learning—"the knowledge of the Latin tongue and some insight into Greek"; and then, "seasoned with the seeds of grace and virtue," he went to court and served "that religious and godly gentleman, Mr. Davison, for several years, when he was Secretary of State." His master found him "so discreet and faithful that he trusted him more than all the others who were round him, and employed him in all matters of greatest trust and secrecy. He esteemed him rather as a son than a servant; and knowing his wisdom and godliness he would converse with him in private more as a friend and familiar than as a master."

Bradford, who was born in 1590, a couple of years after Brewster's service with Davison had ended, must have heard older people describe this relationship, besides Brewster himself, for it seems out of character that the modest Brewster would have talked of his own wisdom and godliness. The wise and godly young man was only twenty-one when, after about four years in Davison's service, Elizabeth's Secretary of State fell into disgrace over his part in the execution of Mary Queen of Scots. Bradford writes that Brewster remained with him through his troubles and for "some good time after," doing him much faithful service, and afterwards went and lived in the country. Bradford does not say where, but he is explicit about the development of the religious group "in the country" and Brewster's part in furthering religion, by practise and example, "procuring good preachers for the places thereabouts, and persuading others to help and assist in such work, generally taking most of the expense on himself—sometimes beyond his means." In another part of his narrative Bradford tells of the subsequent trials and tribulations that led to the exodus to Holland, and of the life of the Pilgrims there. At this point, writing many years later just after the death of the Elder, he sums up the character of his old friend.

"He was wise and discreet and well-spoken, having a grave and deliberate utterance, with a very cheerful spirit. He was very sociable and pleasant among his friends, of an humble and modest mind and a peaceable disposition, under-valuing himself and his own abilities and sometimes over-valuing others. He was innocent in his life and conversation, which gained him the love of those without as well as those within; nevertheless, he would tell them plainly of their faults, both public and privately, but in such a way that it was usually well taken." He was tender-hearted and compassionate with those in misery, especially those who had been of good estate and rank and had fallen into want and poverty, either for religion's sake or through the oppression of others. "None displeased him more than those who would haughtily and proudly exalt themselves, having risen from nothing, and having little else to commend them than a few fine clothes or more means than others."

That there were some fine clothes among the Plymouth settlers we can verify from the Inventories of *Mayflower* Descendants (*The Mayflower Descendant*, Vol. 3, 1901), the men often outdoing the women in wearing bright colors. William Brewster himself owned a violet cloth coat, black silk stockings, a doublet, and an interesting assortment of caps—white, quilted, lace, and violet. To continue with Bradford's character sketch: "When preaching, he deeply moved and stirred the affections, and he was very plain and direct in what he taught. . . . He had a singularly good gift of prayer, both public and private, in ripping up the heart and conscience before God, in the humble confession of sin and begging the mercies of God in Christ for the pardon of it." He thought it better for ministers to pray oftener and divide their prayers rather than to be long and tedious, for heart and spirit, especially in the weak, could with difficulty continue so long to stand bent, as it were, toward God, without flagging and failing. In his office of Elder, concerned with the government of the church, "he was careful to preserve good order and purity both in doctrine and communion, and to suppress any error or contention that might begin to arise."

Before Bradford breaks off his portrait of the Elder, he comments with surprise upon the marvellous providence of God that so many of the Pilgrims lived, like Brewster, to a very old age. "It must needs be accounted for by more than natural reasons, for it is found in experience that change of air, hunger, unwholesome food, much drinking of water, sorrows and troubles, etc., are all enemies to health, causing many diseases, loss of natural vigor and shortness of life." Of all these things, from the time they left England for Holland, where they found both worse air and diet, they had a large part; they had endured a long imprisonment at sea, and crosses, troubles, fears and wants in the new land. They had to frame a new way of living. Brewster took his part and bore his burden with the rest, "living often for months without corn or bread, with nothing but fish to eat, and often not even that. He drank nothing but water for many years, indeed until five or six years before his death; and yet by the blessing of God he lived in health to a very old age." There is a silver beaker in the inventory of Brewster's estate; so one hopes that in his last years it contained something stronger than water.

How surprising survival was, especially at the start, is clear from the vivid account Bradford gives in an earlier part of his narrative, of "the sad and lamentable sickness" that broke out in January and February of the first winter. Wanting houses and other comforts and infected with scurvy and other diseases, they died sometimes two or three a day, so that of one hundred and odd persons, only fifty remained. "And of these in the time of most distres" (to quote from a text with the original spelling, because somehow it creates an atmosphere of greater distress), "there was but 6 or 7 sound persons, who, to their great comendations be it spoken, spared no pains, night nor day, but with abundance of toyle and hazard of their owne health, fetched them woode, made them fires, drest them meat, made their beads, washed their lothsome cloaths, cloathed and uncloathed them; in a word, did all the homly and necessarie offices for them which dainty and quesie stomacks cannot endure to hear named; and all this willingly and cherfully, without any grudging in the least, shewing herein their true love unto their friends and brethren. . . . Two of these 7, were Mr. William Brewster, ther reverend Elder, and Myles Standish, their Captain and military comander, unto whom my selfe, and many others, were much beholden in our low and sicke condition. And yet the Lord so upheld these persons, as in this generall calamity they were not at all infected wether with sicknes, or lamnes."

William Brewster was fifty-four when he sailed on the *Mayflower* and began those twenty-three years of service in the Plymouth Plantation, summed up in the obituary written by his old friend, Governor Bradford. What experiences in his native England and his place of exile, Holland, had made him the attractive and seasoned personality so amiably and affectionately delineated by Bradford?

II

Early Years at Scrooby

When Brewster went to live "in the country" after his service with Davison, it was to the home of his father, another William Brewster, in the village of Scrooby in Nottinghamshire. On January 4, 1575, Archbishop Grindal of York had granted to "our trusty and well-beloved servant William Brewster" the office of "Receiver of our Lordship or Manor of Scrooby and of all liberties of the same in the County of Nottingham." Brewster was also commissioned to the office of "Bailiff of our Lordship or Manor of Scrooby." This office was for life. "We may assume [quoting Dexter, pp. 233–257 *passim*] that at, or about this date, the local legal representative of the archbishop began to live upon the spot where we find him subsequently as an agent of the government as well. There is evidence that he had already resided in the neighborhood for some time, inas-

8

much as, in 1571, one of the same name—with William Dawson and Thomas Wentworth—had been assessed in Scrooby parish, he on property of the annual value of £3." Nothing is known of the mother of the younger Brewster, except her name—Prudence. William Brewster the son was between nine and ten years old in 1575; a plaque in the parish church of St. Wilfred, placed there by the General Society of *Mayflower* Pilgrims in 1955, gives his baptismal date as "c. 1566." Another evidence of William Brewster's age (quoted by Dexter) is a Leyden affidavit of June 25, 1609, where he is said to be aged "about 42," Mary his wife about 40, and Jonathan his son about 16. This would make his birth date "about" 1567. One certain date is that of his matriculation at Peterhouse, Cambridge, December 3, 1580. It was on the statutes of the university that students could not matriculate before the age of sixteen, but there is evidence that they were often younger—as young as fourteen or fifteen.

Wherever in the parish the Brewsters lived before 1575, they probably lived after that date in some housing connected with the Manor of which the elder Brewster was bailiff, for it was certainly a large going concern. Archbishop Sandys of York, who in 1582 followed Grindal (who became Archbishop of Canterbury), held on to it when Queen Elizabeth sought to add it to her estates. He successfully pleaded poverty and she did not insist. (Letter quoted by Dexter.) A few weeks after his letter to the Queen, he made a new indenture

St. Wilfred's Church, Scrooby

of the premises to his eldest son Samuel for twenty-one years; binding him to repair and uphold the premises: manor-house, chapel, bake-house, Brew-house, gallery, barns and stables, and the house standing at the east side of the Great Court, commonly used for the archbishop's offices. Within the moat were kennels, dovecotes, a blacksmith shop, granary, etc. In short, according to

Little Brewster House, Scrooby Churchyard

Dexter, there must have been extensive erections then, which remained much the same for fifty years longer, before being allowed to fall into comparative decay.

Scrooby Palace is described by Leland, the antiquary, as it was about the middle of the 16th century, as "a great manor standing within a moat and builded into courts, whereof the first is very ample, and all builded of timber, saving the front of the hall that is of brick, to the which *ascenditur per gradus lapidis*" (Bartlett, pp. 38–39). Leland calls Scrooby "a meane Townlet," situated in the watershed of the Humber River, near the junction of the rivers Ryton and Idle. The Ryton was once known as Scrooby Water. The Townlet had its parish church, St. Wilfred's, still standing and functioning in the twentieth century, the manor house, and a few cottages and houses of tenant farmers and farm laborers. It was on the main highway from London to Edinburgh—the Great North Road, travelled only by horses, not yet passable for coaches in Brewster's day. But there was much traffic. In 1503 Margaret Tudor, sister of Henry VIII, stopped at the manor on her way north to marry James IV of Scotland. In 1541 Henry VIII slept there for one night, and there Cardinal Wolsey, in disgrace, passed several weeks, about 1529. In 1603 King James I, VI of Scotland, coming south to claim his throne after the death of Elizabeth, paused on April 19 at the nearby town of Doncaster, escorted by the High Sheriff of Nottinghamshire; and his retinue of lords and barons and gentlemen must have made a pretty spectacle for the Scrooby people. James saw enough of the manor to seek, the following August, to get hold of it from the Archbishop of York for the Crown, since he might like to take his pleasure in Sherwood Forest—which lies to the south-west. It would be very pleasant to have the manors of Scrooby and Southwell, "both very well seated for our convenience" in regard to wholesome air and nearness to the place of sport. The king offered a barter deal, but, like Elizabeth, he failed to persuade the archbishop to give it up. A little account of Scrooby in the 16th century, by the Viscountess Galway, stresses the hunting attractions of Scrooby: "It was to Scrooby came their Graces to take their pleasure in hunting the red deer in Hatfield Chase."

From *The England and Holland of the Pilgrims* by Henry M. and Morton Dexter (Boston, 1905), we learn that the elder Dexter visited Scrooby eight times between 1851 and 1887, and to his researches in the neighborhood we owe many interesting details. The manor had been demolished in 1637, except for a farmhouse, left much as it is today (1962). On the outer wall is a tablet placed there in 1920, on the 300th anniversary of the sailing of the *Mayflower*, by representatives of the Anglo-American Society and the Pilgrim Society of Plymouth, Massachusetts. The tablet marks the site of the ancient manor house "where lived William Brewster from 1588 to 1608, and where he organized the Pilgrim Church of which he became ruling elder whence he removed in 1608 to Amsterdam. . . ." The farm—visited by the writer in 1962—was then still in working order, with poultry and cattle, a lovely garden—and eight cats. The elder Dexter, on one of his visits, carried away by permission three oaken beams from the roof of the cow-house, identified as part of the great hall or chapel of the manor. These beams, writes Dexter in a sentimental vein, had echoed to the voices of Bradford, Brewster, Robinson, and Clifton, in the years when the

Separatist church met in the hall; "if the insensate things, when degraded to their present position only could have taken comfort in the thought that a stable and a manger are sacredly historic in connection with the Church of the New Testament" (Dexter p. 249). He adds that the Congregational Library of Boston has a beam and some stone fragments.

But to return to Scrooby Manor in the days when a king and a queen sought to persuade an archbishop to give it to the Crown. The older William Brewster, appointed bailiff of the manor in 1575, also became Master of the Queen's Post at Scrooby and held the post till his death in 1590. Scrooby was the twelfth posting station from London. The post horses were stabled at the tavern that accommodated travellers along the Great North Road; and both the Brewsters—the younger succeeded his father—drew a good income from the tavern. Willison (pp. 15–16) notes that the elder Brewster was a man of "relative affluence" and consequence in the neighborhood, with an income of about £170 a year.

It must have been an interesting place for a growing boy. The countryside was one of woods and fields and streams, good for hunting and fishing. Not for swimming, for as Willison notes, Elizabethans did not swim, and swimming was actually forbidden at Cambridge; they had a "pronounced distaste for water in all its uses." At the posting-station couriers might arrive at any time to deliver a packet or to change horses; only official needs were served. "Every Post in those days was to

Scrooby Manor

keep and have constantly ready two horses at least, with suitable furniture; he was also to have two bags of leather well lined with baize or cotton, and a horn for the driver to blow 'as oft as he meets company,' or four times a mile." (Quote from Viscountess Galway.) Bawtry, only a few miles to the north, was a rendezvous for brigands, and one suspects that a boy would not roam far afield. The tavern must have had some very interesting guests, and we have a few details about what the accommodation was and what it cost. "In a volume published by the Surtees Society is a record of the expenses of Sir Timothy Hutton, on a journey to and from London in 1605. He paid the Post . . . at Scrooby, for post-chaise and guide to Tuxford 10s. and for caudle, supper and breakfast, 7s. 10d., so that he slept under Brewster's roof. On his return he paid 8s. to the Post at Scrooby for conveying him to Doncaster, then reckoned 7 miles, and 2s. for burnt sack, bread, beer, and sugar to wine, and 3d. to the ostler" (Hunter, pp. 68–69). A caudle was a hot drink, made of wine, egg, spices, bread and sugar—very soothing after a jaunt along the Great North Road.

The older Brewster, well-off for the period, could afford to send his son to Cambridge, where he matriculated in December 1580. It is a likely speculation that he owed his admission to the university to the patronage of Archbishop Sandys or his son Sir Samuel, the landlord at Scrooby. The Sandys family turns up again in the Brewster story: Sir Edwin Sandys, another brother, was Treasurer of the Virginia Company and it was with him that negotiations were opened for the settlement in America. An unanswered question is—where did young William pick up enough education to go to the university? Usher says that he was prepared "somehow or other." Dexter speculates about other Brewster names in the neighborhood, picked from this or that record. There was a William Brewster of Bury St. Edmund's in Suffolk who might have been his grandfather, and if so, young William might have attended the grammar school there. But wouldn't there be records? Or there was a

Henry Brewster, vicar of Sutton-cum-Lownd from 1565 to 1598, four miles south of Scrooby, who might have coached him. There is no dearth of Brewsters in the north of England, the name variously spelled,* and as common as the ale and beer they all drank, which some of them must at one time have brewed. And among the "brewers" there must have been "brewsters," women, on the analogy of *spinner-spinster, webber-webster*, and so on. Records in Suffolk, Norfolk, and Yorkshire go back to the 14th century. Of one thing we can be certain: young Brewster must have learned some Latin to be admitted to Peterhouse, and he must have studied it in Lyly's Latin grammar (1513), for Henry VIII had made it "penal for any publicly to teach any other."

* Banks. From the earliest tax lists, Brewsters are found in the Scrooby region and neighboring parishes of Yorkshire. They were taxed in Bawtry, adjoining Scrooby.

III

Cambridge, 1580-1583

Except for the matriculation date we have no direct
information about Brewster during his years at Cambridge, but we have a great deal of detailed knowledge
about life and learning at the university at that time,
and we can imagine Brewster as a part of it. For his
intellectual interests, there is the evidence of the books
in his library. Peterhouse is the oldest of the Cambridge
colleges, its charter granted by Edward I in 1284. "In
the reign of Elizabeth, the Peterhouse Society had become quite considerable, the Buttery books showing the
presence, in addition to Master, Fellows, Bible-clerks
and Poor Scholars, of some scores of paying students."
(Quote Dr. Walker, p. 35.) Legislation of 1581 recog-
nizes the presence, with Fellow-commoners and Pensioners, of Sizars and sub-Sizars. The Master of
Peterhouse from 1554 till his death in 1589 was Andrew
18

Perne, under whom Peterhouse prospered. In 1572 there were 78 names on the Boards, exclusive of Poor Scholars and Servants. In 1581, the roll of persons in Commons had risen to 154. In 1574–5, the college was 8th in the list of 14 colleges, and probably by 1580 was 4th in numbers, coming after Trinity, St. John's and Christ's.

Dr. Perne was a most interesting personality, who must have had a marked influence upon the students in his college, especially since there were few enough, by our 20th century standards, to form a little closed society. He was elected Vice-Chancellor in 1551 and Master in 1554, in the reign of Queen Mary. He seems at that time to have been engaged in discreetly conforming. To quote Pierce (p. 49): "How far his real convictions were involved we may gather from his readiness to shield Whitgift [later Archbishop of Canterbury], then a student at Peterhouse and meditating flight to the Continent, because of his Protestant views. Perne promised to 'winke at him.'" This was during an inquisitorial visit to Cambridge by the Catholic Cardinal Pole. He was (according to Walker, p. 44) "ahead of his age, out of place in a century of persecution. His mind was essentially tolerant." It was not without apparent reason that contemporary wits interpreted certain letters on the weathervane of St. Peter's church as representing "Andrew Perne, Papist" or "Andrew Perne, Protestant," according to the set of the wind. Under Perne, Peterhouse "very fairly represented the surging and conflicting elements of Elizabethan England." (Quote Walker,

p. 46.) Fuller (*Fuller's Worthies*) writes that his memory is to be honored because in the days of Queen Mary "he was the screen to keep off the fire of persecution from the faces and whole bodies of many a poor Protestant." Dexter characterizes Perne as a man who had "gone through the Reformation and what followed with a subtle sagacity, which, under Henry VIII and Edward VI and his two sisters had saved not only Dr. Perne's head but also his prominence." No one was martyred at Cambridge. Still another comment on Perne, from Pierce's *John Penry*, records an amusing student play upon his name: his "credal gyrations" suggested the creation of a Latin verb, *perno*, I turn. But the witticisms were not bitter. He seems to have been a "genuine lover of sound learning and greatly averse from all religious persecution." He was an active promoter of libraries, and a library then occupied the second storey of the western end of the quadrangle, completed in 1450. It was fitted with bookcases, some of the books chained, others free.

What was Brewster taught at Peterhouse and how was teaching conducted? How did he live, and who were some of his fellow-students? How did Town and Gown get along together—or didn't? How did they amuse themselves? In the same autumn of 1580 that Brewster matriculated at Peterhouse, a young Welshman named John Penry also took up residence there. Perhaps he was already there, for Pierce his biographer quotes Walker that Penry's name appears on the bakery

Old Court, Peterhouse, Cambridge

books at Peterhouse on 11 June, 1580. Thirteen years
later this young man suffered martyrdom for his religious beliefs. A very complete *Life, Times and Writings
of John Penry* was published in 1923, written by William Pierce; and in this book we learn nearly everything
that could be found out about Cambridge during the
years Penry was there: courses of study, architecture,
administration, composition of the student body, life in
and around the town—all within the frame of a retro-
spective historical look at the mediaeval university.

The purpose of Peterhouse was to train a secular
clergy and to supply the country with "enlightened and
competent statesmen and administrators." Study of the
Seven Liberal Arts was still university practise: the

Trivium—Grammar, Rhetoric, Dialectic; and the Quadrivium—Music, Arithmetic, Geometry and Astronomy. "The student in Grammar learned to use language, the common instrument of thought; in Logic [Dialectic] he learned to think correctly; and in Rhetoric he learned to convey his thoughts persuasively to others." This for the Bachelor of Arts; and Brewster did not go on, as Penry did, to take the Master of Arts degree. Greek was one of Penry's studies, and we have Bradford's word that Brewster had "some insight into the Greek." Tuition was given by lectures on which the student took notes, to be overlooked by his tutor. "Most of the tutorial work, in the arts course at least, was done by the younger men." Then there were Disputations, defending or opposing a given thesis, the arguments presented in syllogistic form. On display occasions renowned members of the university took part in these debates—sometimes before the Queen herself. "During the forty days of Lent, undergraduates taking their primary degree 'stood' in the schools (lecture halls), prepared to dispute on the given theses with any regent master who chose to test them" (Pierce). Both Oxford and Cambridge, under Elizabeth, had strong chancellors, vigorously Protestant: the Earl of Leicester at Oxford and Lord Burghley at Cambridge. No "Romanism" was taught in the colleges, either openly or secretly—so says Pierce. (Pierce, pp. 36–76 *passim*.)

At Peterhouse there were paying undergraduate lodgers, called pensioners, whose numbers increased rapidly during Elizabeth's reign. Two or three students occupied the same room, younger students being quartered with seniors. A poor student, or sizar, acted as servant to one of the senior Fellows, and slept in a trundle bed. A character in *Return from Parnassus* refers to the time when he was in Cambridge, and lay "in a trundle-bed under my tutor." By paying more, one could choose a better room. The beds, as in a ship's cabin, one above the other against the wall, offered a choice; one could pay an extra shilling or two for a lower berth.

There were two good meals a day and an early breakfast of bread and beer. Dinner was at 11 or 12, supper at 7 or 8, and somewhere in between were a couple of beer-breaks, or biberia; you brought your own drinking cup and had a pint of drink and one-eighth of a half-penny loaf. All details of student life were supervised, and efforts were made to restrain extravagance in dress. Residents were not allowed to keep dogs or falcons in their rooms; "if one can have them in the House, all will want them, and so there will arise a constant howling." A list of creatures not allowed at King's includes, surprisingly, monkeys, bears, wolves, and stags. Perne kept a "cub" in his room for his amusement (cf. V. Woolf— *Those Strange Elizabethans*).

William Brewster and John Penry might have gone together to see the town on market-days. Walking was much favored. Though most games were under a ban, football could be played within the grounds of each college, but there was no college rivalry. Students were warned not to "use or resort to Bull-bayting, Bear-bayting, Common bowling places, Nine-hoals or such like unlawfull games." And it was forbidden to go to the river to wash or swim, the penalty being a whipping by the Proctor. Companies of players, even if they wore the badge of some lordly patron, were discouraged or paid off not to come. The excuse was sometimes the prevalence of pestilence in the place they were coming from. "The very week after Penry's settlement at Peterhouse a company of players came to Cambridge wearing Lord Oxford's badge, and carrying letters of commendaton from Burghley and others. But the Vice-Chancellor and the Heads of the colleges were averse from the proposal, so the actors were fobbed off with a present of twenty shillings towards their expenses, although they protested they had several plays 'already practised by them before the Queen.' Writing apologetically to Burghley, the Vice-Chancellor urged the fact of the hot weather and that the pestilence had not yet vanished from among them; that it was Midsummer Fair time with its crowds of visitors, 'a confluence out of all countries,' some from countries affected by the plague; moreover, and here we have the real reason for the refusal, 'the Commencement time [is] at hand, which requireth rather diligence in study than dissoluteness in plays' " (Pierce, p. 60). The Midsummer Fair was held at Barnwell on the east side of the town and at Sturbridge, two miles from the market-place; where could be seen puppet-shows, rope dancers, drolls, and various strange creatures from "outlandish parts." The Fair was over by September 29.

Dexter (*The England and Holland of the Pilgrims*) tracked down fifteen men who were at Peterhouse in Brewster's time, and others who were at other colleges, whom he may have known. George Johnson, for instance, matriculated at Christ's at the same time that Brewster entered Peterhouse. He had a troubled life of religious dissent, was banished, excommunicated, and died in prison at Durham in 1605. His book on the Ancient English Church in Amsterdam was brought by Brewster to Plymouth Plantation. William Perkins, a Fellow of Christ's in 1582, wrote many works; eleven copies of his treatises were in Brewster's library, and he was author of a catechism later used by the Pilgrims. While the press was operating at Leyden, Brewster reprinted a volume of his sermons. John Udall was at Trinity; condemned to death in January, 1590, he died in Marshalsea prison in 1592. He obtained his B.A. in 1580–81; took holy orders; and as a minister got into trouble preaching Puritan doctrines. Brewster republished at Leyden one of his "seditious" works. Just a couple of years before Brewster came to Cambridge, Dr. Laurence Chaderton preached a famous sermon there— a blast on the abuses of the Church, and this Brewster republished at Leyden.

At Trinity, during Brewster's years at Peterhouse, was the Earl of Essex, who was unlikely to have been one of his companions; but it is interesting, as Willison notes, that "one of the few contemporary historical works to find a place on the shelves of his library at Plymouth was an account of the foolhardy Essex Rebellion, as subtly garbled for official purposes by Francis Bacon" (Willison, p. 34). But Brewster's interest in Essex may date from the phase of Brewster's life that followed his leaving Cambridge after three years, without taking a degree, to enter the service of Sir William Davison. His life then took a new direction for several years, and might have led him into the career of a foreign service official, far removed from that of a religious leader. Bradford's account supplied the clues that patient researchers like the Dexters, father and son, followed up. We may speculate about how it happened that Brewster came to be a member of Davison's household.

IV

In the Service of Sir William Davison, 1583-1588

Early in 1583 Davison was sent to Edinburgh to coun-
teract a scheme of alliance between King James of
Scotland and the French, and the growing strength of
the French interest led to his going back to Edinburgh
in May and June 1584. Suppose young Brewster went
home to Scrooby after the college term in the spring of
1583. He might well have been at the inn and posting-
station on the first of Davison's journeys up and down
the Great North Road, and Davison probably spent a
night or two at Scrooby. "At all events," writes Dexter
(pp. 293–294, *The England and Holland of the Pilgrims*), "the autumn of 1583 and the following winter
seem to have seen Brewster in London as a member of
Davison's household." During the next two or three

years, Davison was a very busy diplomat. There was the
trip to Edinburgh in the spring of 1584, and if the new
member of his household went along, he may have had
a chance to see his family at Scrooby. At the close of
1584 Davison was sent abroad to find out what was going on between Holland and France, and France and
Spain. He had already been in the Low Countries in
1576 and 1577, when he was resident agent at Antwerp;
and in 1579 he had secured a loan for the States of Holland. In April 1585 Davison was ordered home; in August beseiged Antwerp fell, and Davison went to the
fortified town of Flushing, which was temporarily
turned over to Elizabeth, with the keys, which Davison
had in his possession. This is Bradford's story: "The
keys of Flushing being delivered to him, in her majesty's
name, he kept them some time, and committed them to
this his servant [Brewster] who kept them under his
pillow, on which he slept the first night. And, at his
return, the States honored him with a gold chain, and his
[Brewster's] master committed it to him, and commanded him to wear it when they arrived in England,
as they rode through the country, till they came to the
Court." It is intriguing to think of the future Elder and
Pilgrim riding to Court with a gold chain around his
neck.

In January 1586 the Earl of Leicester, at Leyden, was
made Governor-General of the United Provinces, and
Davison was again in Holland, no doubt accompanied
by Brewster, who thus must have seen Leyden years

before he went into exile there. After Leicester's inauguration, Davison left for London, February 14, 1586, having done his part as Elizabeth's representative in her endeavors—as Dexter (p. 294) puts it—to "seem to do something for the Netherlands without doing anything." Davison was soon to have another experience of Elizabeth's intricate political dealings, this time with the problem of Mary Queen of Scots. Brewster, still a very young man of twenty or so, who must by this time have added some worldly wisdom to his godliness, was certainly close to Davison during those months when the Queen was trying to avoid immediate responsibility for the execution of Mary. For the story we shall draw upon the spirited narrative by the late Dame Edith Sitwell in *The Queens and the Hive*.

The final events in the drama of Mary and Elizabeth took place from October to February, 1586–1587. Davison was deeply involved, and we know Brewster was a trusted confidant. We know no details of Davison's establishment, presumably in London near the Court. If one were writing a historical novel, it would be possible to draw upon contemporary sources and create a convincing enough stage setting for Brewster's life in the Davison household during this critical period. One could speculate on what he heard and thought, and on his precise relationship with Davison—a relationship described by Willison as a combination of valet and confidential messenger, and by Dexter as something more than a valet and different from a private secretary. But

Dexter calls it a position of constantly growing value and responsibility. Willison thinks he was no nearer the Court than the servants' hall; but one could guess that this was a very good spot for news; Virginia Woolf, in a flight of fancy in *Orlando*, has Shakespeare listening to the gossip in the servants' hall at Knole. All we know is that Brewster was "there"—like a reporter for a television program, recreating the Reign of Terror or the Battle of Waterloo.

Mary had been tried and condemned, but Elizabeth shied away from ordering the execution, in spite of deputations from the Lords and Commons that came to her at Richmond on November 12 and again on November 24, to demand Mary's death. On December 2 Parliament assembled, the Proclamation against Mary was announced, and people rejoiced, because—in view of the plots to murder Elizabeth that had been uncovered—it had become a question of Elizabeth's survival. It was either Mary or Elizabeth. Mary wrote to Elizabeth on December 19, 1586, a letter that drew tears from her. Leicester and Walsingham felt that delay was dangerous. A new plot was discovered in January. The King of France, Mary's brother-in-law, was shocked only at the manner in which it was proposed to put Mary to death, for since she could so easily be quietly murdered, why offend other sovereigns by executing her? So also thought the Archbishop of Canterbury, who tried to bring Leicester and Walsingham over to his opinion; but they disliked the idea of a quiet murder. On February 1

Elizabeth signed the warrant for Mary's execution and gave it to Davison to take to the Lord Chancellor and have the Great Seal affixed; but as he was leaving the room she complained that Sir Amyas Paulet and Sir Drue Drury, custodians of Mary in prison, had not found any way of putting Mary to death, without Elizabeth's having to sign the death order. She ordered Davison to go to Walsingham and with him compose and sign a letter to that effect, to be delivered to Paulet and Drury (p. 379).

The letter (quoted by Dame Sitwell) states that Her Majesty noted a lack of zeal in them for not having found some way to shorten Mary's life. It argued a lack of love for her, a lack of concern for the preservation of religion and the public good, as well as for their own security, and a disregard for the Oath of Association which they had taken. Why cast the burden upon her, knowing "her indisposition to shed blood, especially of one of that sex and quality"? Davison and Walsingham reported all this in the letter to Mary's custodians, and Davison postponed sending the warrant, not daring to do so without the knowledge of the whole Council. Elizabeth sent for him and asked why he had been in such a hurry to have the warrant sealed. When he asked if he were to proceed, she replied "yes," but lamented that she had not been spared the necessity of making this cruel decision. He protested that the decision must be hers. She ended the audience. Davison, with Sir Christopher Hatton, consulted Burghley—in bed with a "grief in his foot," otherwise gout—and they decided to call a meeting of the Council for the next day. Then they signed a letter ordering the custodians to proceed with preparations for the execution.

Paulet, Drury, Shrewsbury, and Beale (clerk of the Council) discussed the predicament they were in, recalling the prison murders of Edward II and Richard II, and realizing that if they did allow Mary to be murdered instead of legally executed, they would be made scapegoats. And, besides, they really did have some moral qualms, as appears in the letter which Paulet and Drury sent jointly to Walsingham, wherein they complained about being required "by direction from my most gracious Sovereign to do an act which God and the law forbiddeth." "God forbid," wrote Paulet, "that I should make so fowle a shipwrecke of my conscience, or leave so great a blot to my posteritie or shed blood without law or warrant." The Queen was furious at the daintiness and niceness of those precise fellows (pp. 381–382).

The execution took place February 8, 1587, n.s. It is brilliantly described by Garrett Mattingly in his *Armada*. Brewster was definitely not "there," nor was Davison. But the news was all over London when the Earl of Shrewsbury's son brought it from Fotheringhay to Greenwich. The need for a scapegoat was obvious, to save the Queen's reputation in the eyes of Europe, and there was Davison. He was arrested and tried before a commission in the Star Chamber and convicted, March 28, 1587, of "malfeasance through haste"—haste in putting the signed warrant for Mary's execution into effect. He was to be confined in the Tower during the Queen's pleasure and was fined 10,000 marks; but the fine was later remitted and he continued to draw his salary as a Secretary of State. "The beggary of which he later complained was beggary only in a very relative sense," remarks Mattingly. He was lucky, for, as Mattingly also says, "When a Tudor Councillor of Davison's station went through the Traitor's Gate, he rarely emerged in one piece." (*Defeat of the Spanish Armada*, pp. 37–38.) Dexter notes that Davison was ill before his arrest and for a month after, and at his trial he had his left arm in a sling. He obviously needed an attendant and as Bradford records that Brewster did him much faithful service after his disgrace, we can imagine that his service continued during his imprisonment. Prisoners of Davison's standing, when in enforced residence in the Tower were permitted to have a retainer who could go in and out daily, or even lodge within the gates, where rooms were assigned in the Beauchamp Tower. The prisoner had to provide most of his own furnishings and amenities; if he had the money, he could have his meals sent from the table of the Lieutenant-Governor. So there was plenty for a retainer to do, and one likes to think that young Brewster was the person selected, since for more than three years he had been in close and confidential association with Davison. Did they talk over the defeat of the Armada? What was it like in the London streets when the news came?

One thing is obvious: Brewster, still in his early twenties, had received a pretty comprehensive education in the ways of the world of politics and diplomacy in Elizabethan England. Did he regret the abrupt termination of a possible career as a minor officer of some sort in the foreign service? Or did he go back with relief to his father's home in Scrooby? Davison was released in September, 1589. Brewster may have gone North before that time. That he went with the goodwill of Sir William Davison we know from documents connected with his appointment to the Post at Scrooby.

The older William Brewster died in 1590, and his son seems, as one passage in a letter implies, to have helped him in his duties before his death. The recently appointed Postmaster General, Sir John Stanhope, Baron Stanhope of Harrington, wrote a letter concerning Brewster to Secretary Davison, dated August 22, 1590, concerning the appointment to the Scrooby post. A cousin of Stanhope's, Samuel Revercotes, was soliciting the place for an applicant of his. Stanhope had a correspondent, a Mr. Mylls, who kept him informed about Scrooby affairs, and upon whom he relied in this matter of the appointment. To quote Stanhope: "All this whyle, nor to this owre, I never harde one wourde from younge Brewster, he neyther came to me beynge in towne, nor sent to me beynge absent; but as thoughe I were to be overuled by others, maid his waye accordynge to his lykynge." Stanhope, apparently annoyed because Brewster did not seek him out, nevertheless expressed his willingness to redress his error, with

Davison's help, if he were wrong. Stanhope had written letters granting the post to his cousin's candidate, but was willing to revoke the grant, if he could do so without "dysgracynge" his cousin.

Charles Deane read this letter before the Massachusetts Historical Society in May 1871, and appended a footnote: "Mr. Sainsbury, who copied this letter for me, writes that the Earl of Worcester went to Scotland in June, 1590. The office of postmaster on the great roads in those days required him to keep relays of horses for forwarding the letters and to find rest and refreshment for travellers and perhaps aid in facilitating their journey." The letter is endorsed by Davison, and the endorsement appended to the letter, with an explanation supplied by Mr. Deane to this effect: that Sir John was evidently misinformed about Brewster; and the gist of Davison's endorsement was that Brewster had been possessed of the place long before his father's death, as proved by the record of his name among other posts and receipt of the fee for a year and a half; "neither is there any just cause now to except against him either in respect of his honestie, sufficiency for the service, discharge thereof hitherto, or other reasons whatsoever." Moreover he had been "at charge for provision this hard year for the service," and would be at a loss if suddenly dispossessed, "and the example would be harmful."

Thus, as far as we know, the relationship with Davison came to a friendly end. Davison was in retirement in London. He died in the London borough of Stepney in 1608; and we have no record of any journey of Brewster's to London. Brewster was married, 1591, to a girl belonging to a local family: Mary Wentworth, daughter of Thomas Wentworth, who was the older Brewster's predecessor at Scrooby Manor. Mrs. Perle Lee Holloway, of Boulder, Colorado, who is tenth in descent from Elder Brewster, has spent years of research into the ancestry of Mary Wentworth, and has compiled a table of sixty-three families connected with Mary. According to this genealogical tree, Mary was descended from King Edward I, through his fifth son, Thomas Plantagenet of Brotherton, Earl of Norfolk and Marshal of England. Thomas's daughter, duchess of Norfolk, his sole heir, died in 1399, leaving a daughter, Elizabeth, who married John, Lord Mowbray. The line continues, sometimes through daughters and sometimes through sons, until we come to Sir Thomas Wentworth of Wentworth-Wodehouse, who died in 1548 at the age of seventy. He appears to have been an interesting gentleman, so opulent that he was styled "Golden Thomas," and so independent that he paid seven pounds, ten shillings and five pence as part of a fine for refusing knighthood. The value of such a sum in those days must have been very considerable. Why did he refuse? Was there a 16th century racket of some sort in these honors? But later he was knighted for bravery at the battle of the Spurs, in 1513, where Henry VIII routed the French—and where the famous Bayard was taken prisoner. In 1528 Wentworth "obtained license from

Henry VIII to wear his bonnet and be covered in the royal presence." This favor, as recorded in Mrs. Holloway's book, was granted because he was "infirm." Since he did not die until 1548, he had twenty years ahead of him to wear his bonnet.

The Wentworths of Wentworth-Wodehouse had been in possession of this manor from the late 13th century, son succeeding father. The title seems to come and go. The "Golden Thomas" who paid the fine was the son of William Wentworth, who possessed an impressive string of manors; and "Golden Thomas's" son was Thomas Wentworth of Scrooby, Nottinghamshire, who married Grace, daughter of John Gascoigne of Lasing Croft. Mary was one of his four children. The available information about Mary's marriage to William Brewster, bailiff of Scrooby Manor, is summarized in *The American Genealogist*, January 1965, volume 41, number 1. A *Mayflower* Descendant, Franklin Brewster Folsom, who has examined Mrs. Holloway's book, wrote to me that there was "precious little meat on all these old bones." True. But to quote Mrs. Holloway, through Mary's Royal descent, all Brewster descendants become eligible for membership in the "Magna Charta Barons" or "Dames," as the case may be, the "Society of Descendants of Knights of the Most Noble Order of the Garter," and the "Sovereign Colonial Society of Americans of Royal Descent." Mrs. Holloway herself is a Magna Charta Dame.

Mary Wentworth, after her marriage, would have

been too busy to care about her descent from that remote fifth son of Edward I, if she knew anything about
it. She must have superintended and taken an active part
in the business that made the household of that period a
complete self-contained economic unit: brewing and
baking, churning and spinning, cooking and preserving,
caring for the chickens and the doves, tailoring and doc-
toring, and all the other duties. If she could read and
write, as she probably could, belonging as she did to a
family of substance, she would have had precious little
time to practise these accomplishments. And she had
children. A son, Jonathan, was born about 1593, and
there may possibly have been an older son. Where did
the family live? A tablet on a little house, still standing
in back of the churchyard, states that Elder Brewster
lived there from 1594 to 1607. Or they may have lived
some of the time at the farmhouse, all that is now left
of the manor. When Scrooby Manor was flourishing,
there must have been plenty of accommodation for the
bailiff and his family.

Dexter (p. 328) thus sums up Brewster's position at
Scrooby about 1600: "A young husband and father; an
officer of the Queen; residing at Scrooby in the manor-
house of an archbishop; having some university culture
from Cambridge, enlarged by an experience of certain
work at the Royal Court, and broadened by an observa-
tion which had reached into the Tower as well as
extended beyond the narrow seas; refined by some
acquaintance with many good and great men; recog-

nized as religious and influential, and the subject of profound spiritual convictions which gradually were deepening towards the absorption of all the great aims of life. Yet he still was within the communion of the Established Church, and his hands were full of work of various kinds." One may add to Dexter's summary that he had knowledge gained through his association with Davison of the ambiguities and treacheries of the power politics of a troubled period.

Brewster resigned his office of postmaster at Scrooby in September, 1607. What happened during the years from 1590 to 1607 to the religious dissenters in London and elsewhere must have become known to the people at Scrooby and others in the neighborhood along the Great North Road, and certainly influenced the development of the religious movement that had grown strong by 1607. What had been going on? In telling the story since we have no direct information about Brewster, it is convenient to focus attention upon Brewster's fellow student at Peterhouse, the young Welshman, John Penry. Surely Brewster would have heard of his persecution and martyrdom, and would have known the circumstances that led to his tragic end.

V

Puritans and Separatists

About the time, 1589–1590, when Brewster was occupied with taking over his father's duties at Scrooby, attending to the settlement of his father's estate—he died intestate—getting married and starting a new life in his old home, John Penry had also withdrawn to the north, to Scotland, thus avoiding arrest for his suspected part in the secret printing and circulation of certain religious tracts of his own, and of the notorious Martin Marprelate pamphlets, which attacked in satiric and often shockingly scurrilous fashion the bishops of the Established Church. The control of the bishops was in Elizabeth's hands; they were the instruments of her authority to compel religious uniformity throughout her kingdom; and to enhance their authority they were clothed with almost all of the outward pomp that had graced their Catholic predecessors. It is hard for us to realize

40

how furiously the dissenters of whatever sect resented the gorgeous vestments of the new established clergy; they were symbols of the hated Rome.

According to Pierce Penry's feud with the bishops grew out of his passionate concern over the godless condition—as he conceived it—of his Welsh country-men, who had at this time no Bible in their native tongue, who heard only parts of the Gospel read to them in Welsh—merely read, not expounded by prop-erly ordained clergymen, because the bishops neglected the remote parishes. It was bad enough in England, where many parishes were ill cared for, because of the habit of the bishops to hand out livings to their protégés, so that one clergyman had too many to take care of. But it was much worse in Wales. As soon as Penry com-pleted his education at Cambridge and Oxford, he plunged into the fight against the corruptions of the Church. Professor McGinn, in *John Penry and the Marprelate Controversy*, maintains that everything that Penry wrote about the Welsh church is "an echo of the English Puritan attack on the episcopacy" (p. 53). There was a Puritan circle in Northampton where Penry had many friends, including the family of the girl he married. It was not only in London that Non-conformist groups were active in the 1580's and 1590's. They included both Puritans and Separatists, the Puri-tans generally hoping to reform the Church from with-in, and the Separatists seeing no hope except in coming out of the Church altogether. The Separatists took their name from II Corinthians 6: ". . . come out from among them, and be ye separate, saith the Lord, and touch not the unclean thing." Penry was a Puritan until the last period of his short life, after he had returned to London from a three years' stay in Scotland.

How were the reformers to reach the people and make their views known? The restrictions on printing by decree of the Star Chamber are summed up by Professor McGinn: "Any book either printed or published against the Queen's injunctions, ordinances or letters patent was liable to forfeit, and any printer or publisher responsible for such a book as this was to suffer three months' imprisonment and was not to be permitted to print again; the selling, binding, and stitching of secretly printed books was likewise prohibited; finally, the wardens of the Stationers' Company were given power to search all suspected places, to seize all books printed against the Queen's ordinance, and to arrest anyone involved in their printing, binding, or sale" (p. 13). Every printing press in the country was registered; the number of presses in the possession of each printer was limited; religious propaganda—"contraband literature"—thus had to be printed in secret. A certain Robert Waldegrave in London was known as a printer of Puritan works, and it was he who printed tracts for Penry and Udall and the mysterious Martin Marprelate, who was probably Penry himself. According to Professor McGinn: "In addition to the vast amount of circumstantial evidence pointing to Penry as author, proofreader, compositor, and publisher, the fact that these tracts, though presbyterian in content, were separatist in spirit at a time when Penry himself was turning from presbyterianism to separatism forces the conclusion that to him alone belongs the title of Martin Marprelate." If this attribution is accepted, "To Penry then, will be awarded the title already given Martin, namely, that of 'the great prose satirist of the Elizabethan period' " (p. 200).

Pierce in his life of Penry gives a lively picture of the hazards of printing subversive literature in Tudor England. Waldegrave's printing-house in the Strand near Somerset House was raided in April, 1588, and the undelivered stock of Udall's pamphlet, "The State of the Church of England laide open," was seized together with the presses and type found on the premises. "In the confusion of the midnight attack, Waldegrave managed to seize and hide under his cloak a useful fount of pica type, with which he escaped in the dark" (p. 180). When, thirty years later, Brewster had his printing press in Leyden, he may well have recalled the almost legendary tales of the travelling or wandering press in Penry's time. At one point Waldegrave was actually operating overseas in La Rochelle. Penry was much involved in the wanderings of the press, which have some of the fascination of cloak-and-dagger stories.

For instance, a certain Sir Richard Knightley, of Puritan sympathies, had a tenant, a husbandman named Jeffs, who was persuaded to go to the current hiding-place of the press (East Molesey in the neighborhood of Kingston-on-Thames) and convey a "load" to the big house at Fawsley. Sir Richard sent a ring to Penry who was to accompany the load—a ring that would pass him and his cargo into the Fawsley grounds. They made the journey in a heavy two-wheeled broad-tired springless cart, with a couple of stout horses suitable for the rough difficult tracks of Northamptonshire. Penry knew the way, having often covered it on foot; they could go only a few miles a day by unfrequented paths, and they had to find safe lodgings each night. As they drew near Fawsley, Penry went on ahead and presented the ring, recognized by the gate-keeper as his master's. Then along came the cart and the press was lodged in the house. Pierce reports many local legends about the press: "one that it was lodged in a nursery ascended by a spiral staircase; a part of the house not now in existence, or we should be able to judge if a printing press could ascend the stairway." Later, during some of the examinations in Penry's trial, Sir Richard said he had not seen the press, which was at the "town-end" of the house, that is, the servants' quarters. Another little detail pictures Penry, when the press was operating—noisily, one supposes—as distracting attention by sauntering about the grounds in "gallant attire": "a long skye-coloured Cloak . . . and had the Collar of the said Cloak edged with goulde and silver and Silke Lace, and a light coloured Hatt, with an arming Sworde by his side."

"The activity of the bishops," writes Pierce (Book II—Travelling Press. Pg. 193–199, 206–216), "in following the trace of the secret travelling press and in tracking down all concerned in its operations, was incessant." It was persistent enough to determine Penry and Waldegrave to escape and take asylum with the Presbyterians in Scotland. If they were caught in England, the prospect was grim; not merely imprisonment but torture. As Pierce comments, Archbishop Whitgift had had experience of the "efficacy of the rack in unlocking the tongues as well as the knee-joints of his prisoners." Before he set out for the north, Penry "lurked here and there like a fox," seeing his wife and child at Northampton when he could; but he was finally on his way in September 1589. Brewster, journeying back to Scrooby about this time, would have gone openly by the Great North Road, but Penry would travel as unobtrusively as possible by unfrequented ways. At Newcastle-on-Tyne, close to the Border, he stopped briefly at the door of that other Cambridge dissenter and fellow-student at Cambridge, Udall, who was there laboring in the Gospel field, and received advice and information about the rest of the journey and what reception to expect in Edinburgh from the Presbyterians. Their views about bishops were similar to Penry's and there was a tradition of friendliness between them and the Puritans. At this moment, and for a short time thereafter, there was peace between the young King James, newly married to Anne

of Denmark, and his Kirk, though James was stubbornly
for the Episcopacy, as Brewster was to learn to his cost
years later.

Penry and Waldegrave were well received and for a
time wrote and printed quite freely, though it was not
long before the English began to agitate to have these
seditious fellows thrown out of Scotland. In spite of
alarums and excursions, they remained until 1592, and
Penry even had his wife and children with him. The
names of his daughters reflect relative security: Deliverance, Comfort, Safety, Good Hope. But Penry's heart
was always with the religious needs of his Welsh coun-
trymen, and when the harassments grew too annoying,
he returned to London by a circuitous route. His wife
and two of the infants made the very rough voyage by
sea from the Forth to the Thames, and Penry eventually
joined them at Stratford-by-Bow in London's East End,
at the sign of the Cross Keys.

Penry found the Separatist community all astir in London. A Puritan up to this point, he became a Separatist.
To quote Professor McGinn (p. 173): "During the final
two years of his life, Penry abandoned presbyterianism
and became actively involved in the Separatist movement." The group later formed around Brewster at
Scrooby were also considered Separatists; so it is important to be as precise as possible about the distinctions
and differences among the dissenting groups; and to do
that it is necessary to go back a little. Pierce in his life
of Penry has traced that back history. He quotes some

evidence from the writings of William Bradford to prove the existence in London of dissenting communities even before the days of Queen Elizabeth. There was a Secret Church, "formed and sustained in the City, in the days of Bonner and Mary; when the smoke of the torment of the saints rose from Smithfield." It was, says Pierce, a fully organized Church, "furnished with minister and church officers exercising church discipline, administering the Christian sacraments, and caring for its poor," and also for the families of those who were imprisoned and of the martyrs. "They met in no consecrated buildings . . . They thankfully assembled in private houses; at the house of one Brooke, a salter of Queenhithe; at a fishmonger's wife's house, Mistress Barber's, in Fish Street; at the King's Head, Ratcliffe; at a dyer's house at Battle Bridge; at Sir John Garden's at Blackfriars. They found an asylum at an inn in Aldgate, in a cloth worker's loft, in a cooper's house in Pudding Lane; also on board ship at Billingsgate Wharf; and, on several occasions, on board the ship *Jesus*, lying between Ratcliffe and Rotherhithe, where they had prayer, sermon, and the holy communion. They met in great peril . . . In a riverside house in Thames Street, at a service held at night, they had a great deliverance. The house was surrounded by their enemies. In their emergency a mariner of their company 'plucked off his slops and swam to the next [nearest] boat, and rowed the company over, using his shoes as oars.' " The worshippers numbered sometimes forty, sometimes as many as two hundred. One arrest in Mary's time took place at the Saracen's Head in Islington, where they had gathered under pretext of seeing a play, but really to celebrate holy communion. Islington, a flourishing borough of modern London to the north of the City, was then a wooded area, where in 1593 a big haul of later dissenters was made (Pierce, pp. 355–385 *passim*).

The arrangements between Church and State under Elizabeth left the bishops with great power, and retained the vestments and other reminders of the Roman Church. "We may be sure," again quoting Pierce, "that the surviving stout-hearted Protestants, of the Secret Church in the days of Mary, regarded with peculiar distaste this resuscitation of the trappings of the Roman priests. These formed the nucleus of the nonconforming body, which clung to their liberties and their purer faith, and met for separate worship from the beginning of Elizabeth's reign" (p. 314).

The Separatist communities in London were regularized under the leadership of Francis Johnson, a Cambridge graduate of Christ's, 1581. His brother, George Johnson, had been at Christ's when Brewster was at Peterhouse. "Something like a religious revival was quickening the scattered members of the persecuted Church." Quoting Pierce: "They came from all parts of the City, threading their way under most difficult conditions, to their secret meetings, for worship and church fellowship, undeterred by the danger of imprisonment, ruinous fines, and the gallows." Two of their

leaders were in prison, Henry Barrowe and John Greenwood, both executed later, when Penry himself was in
prison awaiting execution. It is important to note that
the authorities distinguished between two classes of
Protestant Nonconformists; though they persecuted
both, those dissenting brethren who were willing to
return to their parish churches, if some little concessions
were made in the matter of Roman vestments and the
sign of the cross at baptism and the like, were recognized
as being in a different category from the new Noncom-
formists. The latter professed a church theory utterly
destructive of Elizabeth's arrangements. The church of
these new Separatists, as they were now being called,
was a self-governing democracy; and the prelates were
not slow in pointing out to Elizabeth that their ecclesiastical polity would have a repercussion upon the political
ideas of her subjects. It meant "popularity," for so they
called the democratic principle. Therefore the members
of this new community were charged with the vague
crime of "sedition." No men of British blood, professing
a Protestant and evangelical theology, the theology of
Elizabeth's bishops, were put to death for their faith.
Those who were put to death, like Penry and Greenwood and Barrowe, all professed the Congregational or
democratic faith and order. The movement toward
separation from the Established Church was hastened
by the consecration as Archbishop of Canterbury of
John Whitgift in 1583. "His accession, therefore,
marked the end of all hope . . . for reform through

appeals to the Queen, to her Privy Council, or to the Parliament" (McGinn, p. 36).

The transition from Popery to Protestantism is too complicated a business to be traced here. Pierce tells the London story with a wealth of fascinating detail, as he follows Penry's progress to martyrdom. One leader of the movement gave his name to groups loosely called Brownists. He was Robert Browne, a controversial figure even today in theological history. He was a graduate of Corpus Christi, Cambridge, a few years before the time of Penry and Brewster; he became a schoolmaster in an East Anglian town from 1574 to 1577, and then was invited back to Cambridge to preach. Pierce calls him a remarkable and original teacher, who wrote two important works, published in 1582: *Reformation without tarrying for any*, described by Dr. McGinn as "the first stirring appeal for separation from the Established Church" (p. 23); and *A Book which sheweth the life and manners of all true Christians*. He did not stay long in Cambridge, where he preached publicly and exhorted people in their homes. But he refused to accept a call or a pastoral charge. It was in the year just before Brewster and Penry entered Peterhouse that Browne was preaching his doctrines openly in a Cambridge pulpit. And Pierce says that Penry moved continually towards Browne's ideals. His later history includes an (at least) outer reconciliation with Archbishop Whitgift in 1585 and the incumbency of a parish in Northamptonshire. There are ambiguities

in this later career, which do not, however, obscure the
fact that his ideas governed groups of dissidents, some of
whom were in Amsterdam when the Scrooby exiles
first arrived in Holland.

Pierce's account of the trials and tribulations of the
London Separatists is peppered with such details as "cast
into prison," "indicted and burned in the ear for a
vagabonde and prest for a soldier," "sent to Bridewell to
grind in the mill." But somehow or other they got their
books and pamphlets printed. "Though Barrowe was in
prison his books were circulated and read . . . And
Greenwood's and Penry's books were possessed by
many." Besides the university men, like the two John-
sons and Penry, there were among the leaders of the
persecuted community scriveners, apothecaries, gold-
smiths, haberdashers, and craftsmen, like shipwrights.
"They attended the meetings of the Church with admi-
rable loyalty, in spite of the difficulties which lay in the
way; walking in the dawn to Islington or Deptford; or
hurrying along the dark wintry streets between four
and five o'clock in the morning, to the schoolhouse in
St. Nicholas Lane, or to Nich. Lee's house in Smithfield. There were sometimes a hundred persons present,
seldom less than sixty. . . . The brethren were very
cautious. The next place of meeting was given at each
gathering, or if by chance that could not be done, a
brother or likely enough a sister, hung around More-
gate and gave the direction." The schoolhouse in St.
Nicholas Lane was probably most frequently selected.

Communion services were held there and baptisms administered and discipline determined. But government spies brought in information, and there were raids in the small hours of the night on the schoolhouse or on the premises of suspected members. Chests and cupboards were ransacked and their contents scattered, during what Pierce calls these "episcopal visitations." "There is no safety to any one of us in any place," as the leading members said (Pierce, pp. 364ff.).

While these often melodramatic events were taking place in London, Brewster, in the service of Sir William Davison until about 1589, was living in the world of diplomacy and politics. When he returned to Scrooby, he must have been very busy becoming acquainted with his duties as bailiff of the Manor, and as innkeeper and postmaster. But his was a listening-post on the Great North Road; and more and more as history moved on into the last decade of the century, he must have heard of the London events, affecting people he had known at Cambridge. The capture, imprisonment, trial, and execution of his classmate, John Penry, took place between March 22 and May 29, 1593. It is a moving chapter in the age-long story of man's inhumanity to man. He was hanged for the crime of "sedition"— whether legally or illegally. Pierce presents the arguments on both sides; they make little difference to the man hanged. But "only by some wire-drawn logic could sedition or treason be even implied." The story of the young Welshman, dragged on a hurdle from the

King's Bench prison to the place where a gallows was erected on the Kent Road, at Thomas a-Waterings, the first halt of Chaucer's Canterbury Pilgrims, moves us after nearly four centuries (Pierce, pp. 446–478). How it must have shocked and saddened William Brewster, remembering their Cambridge years together! One stage of Brewster's life ended with the beheading of a queen. Another turning-point may well have been the hanging of the martyr, John Penry.

VI

Pilgrim Country—Scrooby,
1590–1608

What was it like, up there in the North, in the neighborhood of Scrooby Manor, where the counties of Nottingham, York, and Lincoln meet, and where the movement of religious dissent grew so strong as to threaten the powerful Establishment of that day? A few years ago the Rector of Babworth church near Scrooby became interested in collecting all the information he could about the little group of mainly Nottinghamshire people, who emigrated to Holland in 1607–1608, and some of whom later sailed on the *Mayflower*. The 300th anniversary of that sailing, 1920, had stimulated much investigation into local history and surviving landmarks by such groups as the Pilgrim Society of Plymouth, Mass., the Anglo-American Society, and the General Society of *Mayflower* Pilgrims. Memorial

54

plaques had been placed in St. Wilfred's Church where
William Brewster was baptized and where there is a
Brewster pew; on the little house back of the church,
where he is said to have lived; and on the wall of the
farmhouse—all that remains of Scrooby Manor. The
Reverend Edmund F. Jessup published a small but
valuable monograph, paper-back, *The Mayflower Story*,
in 1957; a second edition, 1962, was placed with other
church publications on a table in the vestibule of the
Babworth church, where the present writer found it in
1962. Another little leaflet, dated 1955 and priced at
sixpence, entitled *The Pilgrim Mothers*, honors the
courage and endurance of those mothers, who had to
endure the same hardships and privations as the Pilgrim
Fathers, and "put up with the Pilgrim Fathers as well"
—as the ancient quip has it. *The Mayflower Story*, which
lists the passengers on the *Mayflower* and contains a
bibliography of the most important source materials, is
dedicated "To Rosemary and William, Little Pilgrims
in the Atomic Age," suggesting thought-provoking
analogies between past and present pilgrimages through a
troubled world. It is pleasantly ironical, considering the
hostility to bishops felt by the Separatists, that *The Mayflower Story* has a Foreword by the Bishop of Taunton,
who tells us that the Rector of Babworth, "as is well
known in North Notts," gave a great amount of time
and trouble gathering the information and "has peopled
our part of England with men and women who live
again in our imaginations."

The picture map on the cover of the booklet shows us Scrooby church steeple just north of centre. A little to the north-east of Scrooby is Austerfield, where William Bradford was born; south of Scrooby is Barnby Moor, marked by "Ye-olde-Bell," and just south of that is Babworth, with its square church tower, where Richard Clifton, or Clyfton, one of the leaders of the Pilgrims, was rector from 1586 to 1605. Over to the south-west a little figure, shooting an arrow, marks Sherwood Forest—Robin Hood, no doubt. East of Scrooby is the town of Gainsborough with its Old Hall, where lived John Smith, another Pilgrim figure; and to the south of Gainsborough is Sturton-le-Steeple, duly supplied with a church steeple, where John Robinson, the pastor of the Pilgrims in Leyden, was born. There are other places—pictured with inns, Norman doors, Saxon churches, spreading oak trees, priories, all having some connection with the Pilgrims, and all inviting us to tour a delightful countryside in a little English car. Bawtry, just a few miles north-east of Scrooby, once the haunt of brigands, is now a pleasant headquarters for a tour, with good inns. Not on the map, to the west and north, was the stronghold of the great Catholic families of England—a fact to remember in placing the Pilgrims within the religious pattern of the early seventeenth century. The city of York, seat of the Archbishop, is not far to the north of Scrooby. Archbishop Hutton of York was a very tolerant Anglican, who died in 1606; his death meant a decline in episcopal tolerance.

Babworth Church

The Rector of Babworth reminds us that in the six-teenth century it was not television but the Bible that brought family and friends together, to be entertained by its stories and fortified by its truths. "From the group study of the Bible," he writes, "there sprang up the practise of family prayer and a form of worship which

. . . was considered by those who took part to be more in keeping with the simplicity of New Testament tradition" than more elaborate services. Many country clergy of the Established Church encouraged these meetings, and one such parson was Richard Clyfton, who came to Babworth in 1586 and whom Governor Bradford characterizes as a "grave and reverend preacher," who under God had been the means of the conversion of many. To take part in the services of Clyfton's church people came from the surrounding districts, and in time both William Brewster and young William Bradford were numbered among the congregation. But by 1604 Clyfton was in trouble with the ecclesiastical authorities and was deprived of his living. And here Brewster stepped in and offered Clyfton and his family a refuge at Scrooby. According to Mr. Jessup, Brewster had been in the habit of going to hear other local clergymen "whose sermons echoed the thoughts and opinions which had been so familiar to him at Cambridge." One of these preachers was John Smith (or Smyth), another Cambridge scholar who had organized an independent or Separatist church at Gainsborough in 1602. Bradford refers to him as a man of able gifts and a good preacher. But eventually he had to leave the country for Holland, and then Brewster's house at Scrooby became the meeting-place of those in the district who desired to worship according to their consciences.

One must remember that harsh penalties were exacted

for non-attendance at the local parish church. "With Clyfton as its first pastor and Brewster as presiding elder, the Separatist Church at Scrooby was formed in 1606." William Bradford, of good family in Austerfield, orphaned young, came to live with the Brewster family in 1606, as virtually an adopted son. Soon after the Separatist group was established at Scrooby, it was joined by John Robinson, a fellow of Corpus Christi, Cambridge, who later took Holy Orders and had a parish church at Mundham in Norfolk, and still later was a Lecturer at Norwich. But he had an uneasy time, attracting too many worshippers to please the authorities, and so at last he joined the Scrooby congregation as teacher, "thereby completing the pattern of church organization acceptable to the Pilgrims, according to their interpretation of I Corinthians, 12, 28" (Jessup). The passage reads: "And God hath set some in the church: first, apostles; secondarily, prophets; thirdly, teachers."

Trouble finally caught up with the Scrooby group, though by comparison with the trials of the London Separatists, they had had a chance for a rather quiet development. In 1607 Brewster resigned, no doubt under pressure, his Postmastership. It is on record that William Brewster and Richard Jackson were served on December 1, 1607, with a process to appear before the Court at York. The charge was Brownism. They gave their word to attend, but did not appear; and in consequence were fined £20, and their arrest ordered, December 15,

1607. The officer charged with apprehending them couldn't find them—a preview of later episodes in Brewster's life. The fines were duly levied for "non-appearance upon lawful summons at the Collegiate Church of Southwell." Reflecting that John Penry and other contemporaries had been imprisoned in the Fleet and sent to the gallows on similar charges, Brewster and his friends decided that they would have to pay the price of freedom in voluntary exile abroad. Holland was the obvious choice. In April 1608, a truce was signed for twelve years between the Netherlands and Spain, which recognized Dutch independence and the right to trade with the Indies, and which guaranteed freedom of worship—except for the Roman Catholics. The truce would end in 1620. So the years between would represent a breathing spell for Separatists, Brownists, and other dissenting sects.

Bradford's narrative of what happened next has the vivid detail of a first-hand report. He was then about eighteen and a member of the Brewster household. He describes the Scrooby congregation as "hunted and persecuted on every side, so that their former afflictions were but as flea-bitings in comparison of these which now came upon them. For some were taken and clapt up in prison, others had their houses beset and watcht night and day, and hardly escaped their hands; and the most were fain to flie and leave their houses and habitations, and the means of their livelihood." They knew not only that there was freedom of religion in the Low

Countries, but also that people persecuted for their religion in London and other parts of the land had already gone into exile in Amsterdam. Their dilemma was made acute by the fact that "though it was made intolerable for them to stay, they were not allowed to go; the ports were shut against them, so that they had to seek secret means of conveyance, to bribe the captains of ships, and give extraordinary rates for their passages. Often they were betrayed, their goods intercepted, and thereby put to great trouble and expense."

In his lively narrative of the frustrating but finally successful attempts at flight from the east coast, Bradford unfortunately does not tell just what roles were played by Brewster, Robinson, and himself; but only, in concluding, says that the principal members were "of the last and stayed to help the weakest over before them." One group arranged with a shipmaster to get passage at Boston in Lincolnshire for themselves and their goods, to be taken on at night at a convenient place. But when he had them and their goods aboard, he betrayed them to officers who took them and put them in open boats and "rifled and ransacked them, searching them to their shirts for money, and even the women further than became modesty; and then carried them back into the town, and made a spectacle of them to the multitude that came flocking on all sides to see them. Being thus rifled and stripped of their money, books, and other property, they were brought before the magistrates, and messengers were sent to inform the Lords of the Council about them." Bradford says that the magistrates used them courteously—which is rather unexpected and pleasant to hear; but had no power to release them until orders came from the Council. After a month's imprisonment, most of them were dismissed and sent back to where they had come from, except for seven of the leaders who were kept in prison and bound over to the Assizes. Among these was Brewster.

The next spring some of the same group along with others made another attempt from a point nearer home. Mr. Jessup is precise about the route to be taken: "The women and children should make their way down Ryton Water to Bawtry and from there down the Idle and Trent to meet their menfolk, who were to walk overland, at a deserted point on the Lincolnshire side of the Humber." "We know," says Mr. Jessup, "that Mistress Brewster had with her a girl of seven or eight and carried an infant just newly born." The daughter had been christened, rather significantly, Fear. Arrangements were made with a Dutchman at Hull who had a ship of his own belonging to Zealand. The deserted point was a large common, writes Bradford, a good distance from any town. Mr. Jessup's version of Bradford's story is a little easier to follow, and we may be sure he checked the geography. "The small boats bringing the women and children arrived first and sought protection from the biting wind in the entrance to Killingholme Creek—now the site of Immingham Dock.

Early the next morning the ship arrived and began to embark the men. Those in charge of the small boats found that they were silted in and stuck fast in the mud. As the next tide released them and the first boat was drawing alongside the Dutch ship"—and here let us take up Bradford's narrative: " . . . the captain of the ship, seeing how things were, sent his boat to get the men aboard who he saw were ready, walking about the shore. But after the first boatful was got aboard and she was ready to go for more, the captain espied a large body of horse and foot, armed with bills and guns and other weapons—for the countryside had turned out to capture them. The Dutchman, seeing this, swore his country's oath, 'Sacramente!' and having a fair wind, weighed anchor, hoist sail and away! The poor men already aboard were in great distress for their wives and children, left thus to be captured, and destitute of help—and for themselves, too, without any clothes but what they had on their backs, and scarcely a penny about them, all their possessions being aboard the bark, now seized." Bradford was on board this vessel.

They had a terrifying fourteen days' stormy passage, during which they were driven close to the coast of Norway. Bradford modestly lays little stress upon the prayers and the courage of his company—"even when the water ran into their mouths and ears"—and the sailors were crying "we sink! we sink!" They called on the Lord and in the end reached the desired haven. The men left behind on shore managed to escape, except for those who stayed to help the women, who, with their children, were apprehended and hurried from place to place and justice to justice. To imprison them seemed even in those days unreasonable, to send them home impossible because they had no homes to go to; so "after they had been turmoiled a good while, and convoyed from one constable to another, they were glad to be rid of them upon any terms, for all were wearied and tired of them." Just how they got rid of them Bradford does not say, except that in the end necessity forced a way for them. Mr. Jessup thinks that the authorities connived at their departure for Holland. Because of all these public troubles, their cause became famous, and "occasioned many to look into the same," and their goodly carriage and Christian behavior left a deep impression upon the minds of many; and eventually, some at one time and some at another, some in one place and some in another, they all crossed over by the end of 1608. Pastor Robinson's words, quoted by his biographer, Burgess, are a fitting conclusion to this tale: "For our country we do not forsake it, but are by it forsaken, and expelled by most extreme laws and violent prescriptions, contrived and executed by the prelates and on their own behalf." And so they came to Holland, to live in exile for a dozen years, and then, when the truce with Spain came to an end, and with it religious freedom, to be forced to seek another haven. As Bradford phrased it they knew when they left Holland that they were pilgrims.

Before telling the story of their years in Holland, it is

worth while to examine the concept of religious freedom which the Pilgrims held. Dr. McGinn, after completing his account of the Marprelate Controversy,
reminds us of what religious freedom meant to Penry
and the dissident groups. Puritans and Separatists alike
were scarcely apostles of freedom of thought. "They
wished to worship in their own way, but they wished
also, and perhaps quite as much, to prevent others from
worshipping in any different way. . . . The idea of
'pluralism' in religion is a strictly mid-twentieth century
intellectual and spiritual achievement." One might
suggest, in passing, with the world news of 1969 fresh
in mind, that "achievement" is too positive a word.
"Aspiration" might fit the facts better. Dr. McGinn,
quoting a Presbyterian authority, goes on, however, to
note that the Puritans, like many other religious and
political rebels against despotism, "unconsciously helped
to hasten the realization that if one group is to be free
from molestation it must permit others the same freedom. . . . The Puritans were allied with Jesuits, Huguenots, and Dutchmen in the struggle against the forces
of absolute monarchy and the tyranny of civil power,
and in spite of themselves they contributed to the
furtherance of both civil and religious liberty." When
Penry is described as "an enemy of tyranny, his contribution to religious and intellectual freedom must be
regarded as purely fortuitous." (McGinn, pp. 203–
205 *passim.*) Forget liberty for the moment and think
only of tolerance. "It is incontestable," writes Dr.

McGinn, "that Penry's separation from the Established Church was not a move toward greater tolerance." Browne—and remember that the Scrooby group were called Brownists—recommended placing the power to excommunicate in the hands of every member of the congregation, and that caused the break-up of several Brownist communities; for "apparently the zeal of some of the saints to ferret out the sinners in their midst resulted in even greater intolerance than that experienced under the bishops or the presbytery." The Scrooby Separatists observed some of the consequences of this zeal when they arrived in Amsterdam. Keeping in mind this pertinent comment on the meaning of tolerance and freedom, it is yet fair to rely on Bradford's testimony, quoted earlier, as to the character of Brewster, and conclude that he, at least, was neither intolerant nor vituperative, as were many of his contemporaries.

VII

Amsterdam and Leyden,
1608-1620

The first experience of the Pilgrims in exile was in Amsterdam. As Bradford tells it, the prospect was forbidding: "Having reached the Netherlands, they saw many fine fortified cities, strongly walled, and guarded with troops of armed men; and they heard a strange and uncouth language, and beheld the different manners and customs of the people, with their strange fashions and attire—all so different from their own plain country villages wherein they were bred and had lived so long, that it seemed they had come into a new world. But these were not the things they gave much attention to. They had other work in hand, and another kind of war to wage. For though they saw fair and beautiful cities, flowering with abundance of all sorts of wealth and riches, it was not long before they saw the grim and grisly face of poverty coming upon them like an armed man, with whom they must buckle and encounter, and from whom they could not fly, but they were armed with faith and patience against him and all his encounters; and though they were sometimes foiled, yet, by God's assistance, they prevailed and got the victory." The armed man Poverty with "the grim and grisly face" is like a figure out of a book not yet written —*Pilgrim's Progress.*

Brewster was no stranger to the Low Countries, but his visits there as Sir William Davison's servant-secretary were two decades in the past. The problem of ordering their church affairs concerned Brewster and Robinson quite as much as the problem of earning a living. They found two exiled religious communities already living in Amsterdam: one from Gainsborough under John Smith; and another, larger, led by Francis Johnson of London. Johnson's was one of the earliest and largest of the Separatist congregations of the period, drawn from many parts of England and known as the Ancient Brethren. They had, writes Mr. Jessup, sufficient resources to have completed a fine meeting-house in the heart of the city—"situated in a narrow street which is still known as Brownists' Alley." Clyfton's and Robinson's group became loosely connected with the Ancient Brethren, but though, as Bradford says, there were many worthy men among them, the association turned out unhappily because of dissensions and scandals among the Ancient Brethren. Many members of the congregation were withdrawing, and John Robinson persuaded the Scrooby group to move to the city of Leyden—and just in time.

Bradford is vague about the scandals, but from other sources we learn some intriguing details, recounted by Mr. Jessup: "Elder Daniel Studley found it difficult enough to justify his concealed presence behind a linen basket in the bedroom of the attractive Mrs. Judith Holder, but when Geoffrey Whittaker, another of the Brethren, was found abed with the same lady, his explanation that he had only come to comfort the sick woman and keep her warm was stretching brotherly love beyond endurance. Quite a different construction was put upon the bedchamber incidents by the more responsible leaders of the troublesome congregation. Robinson, the ever watchful and faithful shepherd, had seen that 'Ye pure and unspotty'd Lambes of ye Lord' had fallen into a very unsavoury fold." Elder Daniel Studley was lucky to escape Sir John Falstaff's experience with a linen basket. Richard Clyfton, tired and disappointed, "decided he could go no further along the Pilgrim path," and remained in Amsterdam, where he died in 1616. But the Scrooby group with their pastor, Robinson, and their Elder, Brewster, applied formally to the Leyden civic authorities for permission to settle in Leyden, and were accepted as residents in 1609. There was an attempt by James I through his ambassador, Sir Ralph Winwood, to interfere, by denouncing the group as "ill-conditioned Brownists, not submissive to King and Hierarchy," banished men who deserved no sympathy. But the magistrates refused to consider the charge. Their fine statement is printed in *The Pilgrim Fathers in Holland*, published in Leyden in 1920. The new settlers numbered about one hundred, some disgusted Ancient Brethren having joined them.

Bradford records that "being settled here, they fell to such trades and employments as they best could, valuing peace and their spiritual comfort above any other riches whatever; and at length they came to raise a competent and comfortable living, though only by dint of hard and continual labor." About two years after their arrival they purchased a house in Bell Alley, Klok Steeg, to be used partly as a meeting-house and partly as a home for their pastor. On the small plot behind it, they built twenty-one little cottages, which housed families with familiar Pilgrim names—Allerton, Fuller, White, Jessop, Brewster (Jonathan).

So the Scrooby exiles were accepted in Leyden. For Brewster and Robinson there was the attraction of the University of Leyden, which bestowed honorary membership upon Robinson in 1615. He preached and taught and engaged in theological controversy with the Arminians, who, writes Bradford, "molested the whole state, and this city in particular. . . . So there were daily hot disputes in the schools thereabouts, and the students and other learned people were divided in their opinions between two professors of divinity, the one daily teaching in favor of the Arminian faction, and the other against it. Things grew to such a pass, that few of the followers of the one professor would hear the other teach." Bradford praises Robinson for his habit of listening to both and becoming so well grounded in the controversy that he "began to be terrible to the Arminians," and the preachers of the city persuaded him to dispute publicly with Episcopius, the Arminian professor; he did so on several occasions and foiled his adversary, and so the truth—from Bradford's standpoint—had a famous victory.

And what was it all about? Holland had for some years been the scene of theological disputes. Jacobus Arminius, professor at the university, had died in 1609; his successor, Episcopius, carried on certain anti-Calvinist tendencies—opposing a conditional to an unconditional predestination. In more impressive terminology, the Arminians were supralapsarians rather than infralapsarians: i.e., making the divine decree succeed the Fall rather than precede or determine it. They believed that Christ had made atonement for the sins of all mankind and that all had enough freedom of will to accept that salvation. Arminius, says the *Encyclopaedia Britannica*, was constitutionally averse to narrow views and enforced conformity. From what I can understand about the issues at stake, I fear I am on the side of Arminius and Episcopius, and yet both Robinson and Brewster, gentle men, still found it possible to believe in what seems to many of us today an atrocious doctrine. It is

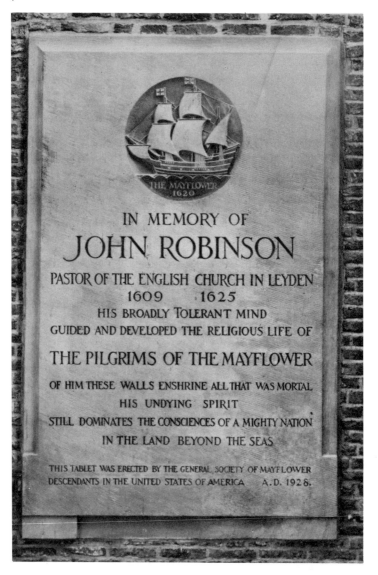

IN MEMORY OF
JOHN ROBINSON
PASTOR OF THE ENGLISH CHURCH IN LEYDEN
1609   1625
HIS BROADLY TOLERANT MIND
GUIDED AND DEVELOPED THE RELIGIOUS LIFE OF

THE PILGRIMS OF THE MAYFLOWER

OF HIM THESE WALLS ENSHRINE ALL THAT WAS MORTAL
HIS UNDYING SPIRIT
STILL DOMINATES THE CONSCIENCES OF A MIGHTY NATION
IN THE LAND BEYOND THE SEAS

THIS TABLET WAS ERECTED BY THE GENERAL SOCIETY OF MAYFLOWER
DESCENDANTS IN THE UNITED STATES OF AMERICA   A.D. 1928.

THE MAYFLOWER
1620

well to remember that the daily struggle to make a living in a strange land was enlivened and given ultimate meaning by these theological excitements; and that people were willing to suffer all things rather than give up their beliefs in what seem to many of their descendants very odd doctrines. Probably our descendants will find some of our political convictions equally odd and grotesque.

While the life of the mind went on at the university, the struggle with that armed man Poverty was gradually successful, in the friendly atmosphere of Leyden, where the exiles received "good acceptation." If they were known to be of that congregation, says Bradford, the Dutch would trust them in any reasonable matter when they wanted money, because "they found by experience how careful they were to keep their word and saw how diligent they were in their callings; and they would even compete for their custom and employ them in preference to others." The Scrooby group and others who from time to time joined them numbered 298. (Banks, *English Ancestry and Homes of the Pilgrim Fathers*). The English colony was much larger, over six hundred. The city records disclose that the English residents engaged in over fifty different occupations, including manual labor and various skilled crafts. Leyden had a flourishing woollen industry, the weaving done at home with hand loom and spinning wheel. Some of the occupations of those who later came to the New World in the four ships—the *Mayflower*, the *Fortune*, the *Anne* and the *Little James*—were these: tailor, fustian weaver, ribbon maker, hat maker, merchant, wood carver, printer. In the Leyden colony were such craftsmen as woolcombers, felt makers, bombazine weavers, cobblers, cutlers, drapers, glovers, brewers. Whatever Brewster's ancestors had done in the way of brewing, that occupation belonged to the past. Brewster's son Jonathan became a ribbon maker and Brewster himself a printer and a tutor in the English language.

The little company of Scrooby exiles settled around Pieterskerk in a quarter of crowded lanes and alleys, where many university students lodged. The Brewsters lived in Stinksteeg—Stench Alley or lane, dark and damp. A Brewster child died there and was buried in St. Pancras, June 20, 1609. The house was called the Green House and was near the Green Gate, where the congregation met for services in Bell Alley. Brewster began to teach English to students and others, drawing up rules to learn it after the Latin manner, as Bradford says. But before long the need arose to print some of the exciting theological material, for Robinson was encouraged not only to preach and dispute, but to print as well. But how to manage it? The problem that had confronted John Penry and the London dissenters faced the Leyden group, because what they printed they wished to circulate in England, where the bishops still had absolute power to censor the press. Part of the problem—printing the material—was solved in 1616, when Brewster set up a printing press in his house, with the financial help of Thomas Brewer, an Englishman from Kent, and with a master printer, John Reynolds, brought over from England. As managing director, Brewster also had an assistant, young Edward Winslow, who had recently joined the congregation. The harmless books and treatises which were first printed bore the imprint of the Leyden Choir Alley Press; and such a book as *A Plaine and Familiar Exposition of the Tenne Commandments* would easily pass the episcopal censor. And so they got under way. (Burgess, *Life of Robinson*, and Harris and Jones, *The Pilgrim Press*.)

The Pilgrim Press has been thoroughly investigated in recent years and has a book all to itself: *The Pilgrim Press: bibliographical and historical memorial of the books printed at Leyden by the Pilgrim Fathers* (i.e., by William Brewster and his associates, with a chapter on the location of the Pilgrim Press in Leyden by Dr. Plooji). By James Rendel Harris and Stephen K. Jones, Cambridge, Heffer, 1922. This book has a photograph of Brewster's Printing House as it was in 1922 and maps showing the position of the house; and included are the title pages of publications, numbers 1–14 and 16–20, with sample pages of text. The address of the Brewster house was, we recall, in Stinksteeg. Research has established pretty clearly that it was an L-shaped house, with two entrances, on Stink Alley and on Choir Alley.

The Separatists had operated a press at Amsterdam under the direction of Giles Thorpe; and Burgess, John Robinson's biographer, speculates that Robinson in Leyden had read and corrected for this press before Brewster and Brewer started their own. In the Brewster establishment, which must have been a very limited one, "the fight for freedom was fought under the cover of secrecy" for three years. Burgess mentions among the first of the volumes printed at the new press a controversial work in Latin by William Ames, 1617, "apud Gulielmum Brewsterum in Vico Chorali" (Choir Alley). But it was one thing to publish under license for sale in Holland and quite another to print books to be "vented underhand in His Majesty's Kingdom." An example of the prohibited books printed by Brewster and Brewer is number 15 (listed in Dexter's Appendix):

The Second Part of a Plain discourse of an unlettered Christian, wherein by way of which he doth ground upon, in refusing conformity to kneeling in the act of receiving the Lord's Supper. By Tho. Dighton, Gent (1619).

As this title rather obscurely suggests, there were among the brethren innumerable points of doctrinal dissension, involving definitions, deviations, and splinter groups. Modern ideological parallels come to mind.

It was probably in the autumn of 1616, to quote Burgess (ch. XVII), that Brewster began this venture, for on October 22, 1619, Carleton (English ambassador at The Hague) wrote that Brewer "for the space of these three years hath printed prohibited books and pamphlets." Brewer must have been an interesting person, judging from his later history; he became a Fifth

Monarchy man, holding advanced views about the approaching End of the Age. He was a member of the University of Leyden and as such had privileges Brewster did not have. But Brewster was a popular private tutor and there was "no lack of rapport between Leyden University and the little English colony of exiles" (*Pilgrim Press*).

There are some speculations about the printing press that are intriguing. A garret in Brewster's house could easily conceal type cases and types. But what of the press itself? During a storm on the voyage of the *Mayflower*, one of the main beams of the ship became "bowed and cracked"—that is, buckled. A great iron screw was got up from the hold and used to jack up the beam, restore it to horizontal, and then fortify it by a post put under it and set firm in the lower deck. Bradford refers to this great iron screw which "the passengers brought out of Holland." Was it part of the printing press? One recalls the adventures of the Wandering Press in the Penry story.

VIII

From Leyden to the Mayflower, *1617-1620*

The approaching end of the truce between Spain and
Holland meant the end of the breathing space for the
seekers of freedom to worship. As Bradford puts it,
"The twelve years of truce were now out, and there
was nothing but beating of drums and preparing for
wars." Burgess quotes from a letter dated December 15,
1617, from Leyden, signed by Robinson and Brewster,
concerning the possibility of establishing a colony in the
New World, and supporting the idea that the Leyden
group was of the right stamp to found such a colony.
The letter is addressed to Sir Edwin Sandys, treasurer
of the Virginia Company and son of that archbishop of
York who had appointed Brewster's father bailiff of
Scrooby Manor. What were the qualifications of the

Leyden group, as Brewster and Robinson set them forth? They believed the Lord was with them; "we are well weaned from the delicate milk of our mother country, and inured to the difficulties of a strange and hard land"; they were as industrious and frugal—"we think we may safely say"—as any in the land; they were not easily discouraged, and they knew their entertainment in England and Holland and knew that they would greatly prejudice both their arts and their means by removal; they could not hope, if they gave up, to recover their present helps and comforts in any other place during their lives, "which are now drawing to their periods." In other words they could be counted upon to stay put, if they founded the colony (Burgess, pp. 214–215).

Sandys got the Secretary of State, Sir Robert Naunton, to sound out the king about this enterprise. To quote Mr. Jessup: "James was interested enough in the idea of a colony which would extend his dominions, but unwilling to make public his approval of an expedition proposed by those who had already left his jurisdiction by stealth. The Pilgrims were represented in this application by John Carver, a merchant of Leyden who had become a member of Robinson's Church. Carver, destined to become the Governor of Plymouth Plantation, was born at Doncaster and had married Catherine White of Sturton-le-Steeple, Robinson's sister-in-law. The other emisary was William Brewster. The King, who had threatened fifteen years earlier, 'I will make them

conform, or harry them out of the land,' must have
mellowed a little with age. He went so far as to ask their
intention and when told that it would be, '. . . the advancement of His Majesty's dominions and the enlarge-
ment of the Gospel by all due means,' he declared that
this was 'a good and honest motion.' Inquiring further
how they proposed to live, he was told that they would
depend chiefly upon fishing. 'So God have my soul!'
replied the King, ' 'tis an honest trade. It was the
apostles' own calling,' and with that, promised not to
hinder the enterprise."

Robinson and Brewster, writing from Leyden January 27, 1618 (n.s.), to Sir John Wolstenholme in London, sent an explanation of certain points of doctrine
and practise raised by some members of the Privy Council. A passage is worth quoting from the briefer of two
declarations enclosed in the letter:

As regards the ecclesiastical ministry, namely of pastors for
teaching, elders for ruling, and deacons for distributing the
church's contribution, as also for the two sacraments—
baptism and the Lord's supper—we agree wholly and in all
points with the French Reformed Churches, according to
their public Confession of Faith.

(Bradford, p. 39)

They add that they are willing to take both the Oath
of Supremacy and the Oath of Allegiance, the first
acknowledging the king as Supreme Head of the Church
of England, and the second pledging civil obedience.

Officers of the Virginia Company thought that they could obtain a grant of freedom of religion from the King, but it proved impossible, in spite of the fact that many of high standing used their influence—among them Secretary Sir Robert Naunton. It did seem probable, however, that the King might "connive at them," if they behaved peaceably; but to allow a claim to religious freedom under his seal—that was something else again. So the messengers brought back word from London to Robinson and Brewster in Leyden that the officials did not think the congregation would be troubled if they went ahead with the undertaking. Several of the congregation thought this a sandy foundation to build on, "but some of the chief members thought otherwise," and advised going ahead, believing that the King would not molest them, even though "he could not confirm it by any public act. And it was further contended that if there was no security in the promise thus intimated, there would be no great certainty in its further confirmation; for if, afterwards, there should be a desire to wrong them, though they had a seal as broad as the house floor, it would not serve their turn, for means would be found to reverse it." As one of the chief members, Brewster may have relied upon his memories of diplomacy, when in the service of Davison, to advise trusting to God's providence for the outcome. So they decided to close with the Virginia Company and procure a patent with as good conditions as possible.

Unluckily just at this moment one of the major subversive activities of Brewster's and Brewer's press came to light. When King James heard that copies of *The Perth Assembly* had been smuggled into Scotland, and that the printing had been traced to the press in Leyden, he was furious and ordered his embassy in Holland to apprehend the operators of the press that was stirring up sedition and schism in his kingdom. And what was this seditious document? In 1619 a Scotsman appeared in Leyden with some manuscripts he wished to have privately printed, and Brewster and Brewer undertook the job. James was bent on enforcing episcopacy in Scotland, and pressed his plans at the General Assembly of the Kirk in Perth in August, 1618. David Calderwood, resenting this plan, as a militant Presbyterian, wrote the tract, *The Perth Assembly*, and also a Latin treatise on the government of the Scottish church. The Pilgrim Press printed the documents and copies were smuggled over into Scotland in April, 1619, packed in vats as a consignment of French wines and strong waters. By June 1619 the pamphlets were in general circulation. Calderwood, who had been hiding in Edinburgh, fled in August to Holland. He had been in Leyden before, when he turned over his mss. to the press. Uncertain as the dates are, we get the impression that Calderwood was a successful commuter between Edinburgh and Leyden. James was not surprisingly angry at the news that Calderwood was in Holland and referred to him as "that knave who is now loupin oversea, with his purse well filled by the wives of Edinburgh." The Edinburgh bookseller when arrested denied having any share in the publishing, but admitted that Calderwood had occasionally slept at his house.

The source of the pamphlet was discovered by the English ambassador at The Hague, Sir Dudley Carleton, who stated in a despatch, July, 1619, that it was printed by "a certain English Brownist of Leyden." He mentioned other publications printed by William Brewster, a Brownist, who "is now [the despatch is dated July 22] within these three weeks removed from thence and gone back to dwell in London; where he may be found and examined." According to Burgess, "we know from other sources that he was there in May of this year, along with Robert Cushman." Cushman and Brewster were negotiating about establishing that colony in America. On May 8 Cushman wrote to Leyden friends that "Mr. B. is not well at this time; whether he will come back to you or go into the North I yet know not." When sought for at the end of July he could not be found. Letters kept passing between Carleton in Holland and Sir Robert Naunton in London. Naunton wrote in a letter of August 3, "I am told William Brewster is come again for Leyden; where I doubt not that your Lordship will lay for him if he come thither; as I will likewise do here; where I have already committed some of his complices and am commanded to make search for the rest." On both sides of the North Sea, then, a sharp watch was kept for Brewster. His name disappears for the time from the list of those actively promoting the plan for emigration. "Carver, Cushman, and Christopher Martin were left to attend to the public business which that plan entailed" (Burgess, pp. 168–169). Brewster, like his old classmate John Penry years before, was "on the run."

Despatches continued to pass between Ambassador Carleton and Secretary of State Naunton, and there were also communications to and from the University of Leyden authorities, some of them concerning that Kentish gentleman, Mr. Thomas Brewer, who, having matriculated at the university, was privileged and had to be handled with care. He was finally persuaded to go to England with the protection, much to the King's annoyance, of a safe-conduct. Brewster, if caught, would have had no special privilege. About these matters there were touchy relations between the Dutch States General and the University of Leyden, and between James I and the Prince of Orange. The ambassador wanted to please James and so his despatches put the best face upon a situation that was full of frustrations. The ambassador, by the way, had had his own troubles in the past, having (so the *Encyclopaedia Britannica* says) been associated, as secretary to the Earl of Northumberland, with the Gunpowder Plot; but he had succeeded in clearing himself, and from 1616 to 1625 he held the post of ambassador successfully. He must have known his way around. His correspondence is "remarkable for its clear, easy, and effective style." But the diplomats did not succeed in catching Brewster—whom the Reverend Jessup amusingly nicknames "the Pimpernel of the Pilgrim Press."

Brewster was actually in Leyden in September, 1619, where lukewarm action was taken against him by the Council of the Provincial State of Holland; he went voluntarily to the "Debtor's Chamber" but was not detained. Sir Dudley Carleton wrote to the Secretary of State: "In my last [Sept. 10] I advertised your Honor that Brewster was taken at Leyden: which proved an error in that the Scout [bailiff] who was employed by the Magistrates for his apprehension being a dull, drunken fellow took one man for another." Burgess comments that this story was good enough for King James. But it looks as if the Leyden authorities were less than eager in the chase. Meanwhile the types of the press were seized, and Brewster kept out of the way. Both the civil and the academic authorities were friendly to this popular private tutor, and so were the students, who "raised a disorder over him and cried 'privilege' "—which he did not in fact have. And presently he slipped off to England under a disguised name—a disguise "patent to the Leyden officials but unintelligible to the English pursuers" (*The Pilgrim Press*).

During the hunt for Brewster, Carleton, following a false clue in September, 1619, made inquiries in Amsterdam, though it seems unlikely in view of the disputes with the Ancient Brethren that Brewster would take cover there. "If he lurk here for fear of apprehension," Carleton was told, "it will be hard to find him." And he was not found. Burgess, Chapter XVII from p. 169 on,

tells a complicated story documented by despatches
from London, The Hague, Leyden, between Naunton
(Secretary of State), Carleton (the English Ambassador) and Leyden authorities.

The various authorities upon whom one relies for this
story indulge in some intriguing speculations about disguised names. It was, for example, the Dutch custom
to use patronymics, and Brewster could have been
known as Master Williamson. This name appears as
joint-executor of the will of a certain William Mullins,
who died in the first winter at Plymouth. "Williamson"
also appears in other connections but has not been identified. Possibly Brewster in this period of being pursued
used the name at Delftshaven, Southampton, and Plymouth, England. It is a plausible speculation. Less plausible, but more picturesque, is another suggestion.
Through Sir Edwin Sandys a patent for a Virginia
colony was obtained, with Brewster's name on it, and
then withdrawn. A new patent was obtained with the
name "Master Wincob" on it, but this, too, was withdrawn, and when still another was prepared, Wincob
had disappeared. Now Wincob or Wencob is Brewster
done into Dutch—wijn koop, or wine merchant. But
wine is not brewed, and Wincop or Whincop is a possible English name, deriving from *whin* or bushes, and
cop or hill—a hill covered with bushes. I fear we shall
have to let Mr. Wincob vanish into the bushes; or accept Bradford's identification—"a religious gentleman
then in the service of the Countess of Lincoln," who

intended to go with them to the New World, but never did.

Brewer meanwhile is referred to in a January 14, 1620, despatch from Naunton to Carleton: something had been drawn from Brewer that in part contented His Majesty, "who bade me tell you that he gives no credit to this fool's confident and improbable assertions; and that he will be very good friends with you, if you can procure Brewster to be taken, wherein he makes no doubt of your careful endeavor." But Brewster was not "procured," and Brewer was finally discharged (Burgess). During all this year while Brewster avoided being procured for King James, preparations were going on for the great colonial adventure, and he must have continued to have some part in the negotiations, whether he was in London or in the North. Pastor Robinson in a letter (June 14, 1620) to John Carver refers to Brewster in connection with Thomas Weston's withdrawal of his capital from the venture. He wonders if Weston "hath thought by withholding to put us upon straits, thinking that thereby Master Brewster and Master Pickering would be drawn by importunity to do more." Burgess comments that Brewster must have been ready to give substantial aid to the enterprise. But where was he? (Burgess, p. 186).

Perhaps in the City, where in Penry's day, a couple of decades earlier, the little secret groups of dissenters used to meet in a cloth worker's loft or a cooper's house, in Pudding Lane or Fish Street. In Aldgate Ward, in the East End, Edward Southworth—one of the merchants interested in the projected colony—had an address in Duke's Place at Heneage House. Robert Cushman, chief of the Merchant Adventurers, wrote to him there a long letter, quoted by Bradford. Heneage House must have been whatever was left of the town palace of the Abbots of Bury St. Edmund's, a flourishing centre in the Middle Ages; it had passed from the abbots into the hands of Thomas Heneage. It stood in the parish of the Priory of the Holy Trinity, but the priory had been dissolved in 1531 and the house granted to Thomas, Duke of Norfolk. Hence the name Duke's Place. The late Elizabethan chronicler, John Stow, describes "the fair courts and garden plots" of the priory, but notes that the area had become "utterly destitute of any parish church." This was a bit of good fortune for the Separatists in the parish, enabling them to escape indictment under the act enforcing attendance at the parish church. But if there were no church? No new church was consecrated on the site until 1622 (Burgess, p. 257, n. 1). A map of the period shows the location of Heneage House near Houndsditch. The site in present-day London is covered by warehouses and business buildings, but the name Heneage still marks an obscure lane.

The Aldgate Ward was the home in the early 17th century of hundreds of Dutch craftsmen, members of the same religious organizations that had welcomed the Scrooby exiles to Holland. As early as 1600 there were also French Huguenots escaping from persecution. But the fine houses had become tenements. Near Heneage House in Brewster's time—and still standing in our day— was the church of St. Andrew Undershaft, a name one associates with Shaw's *Major Barbara*. And in the same ward was the guild-hall of the Ironmongers Company to which Thomas Weston belonged, the merchant concerned with the financing of the *Mayflower* voyage. From the parishes of St. Leonard's Shoreditch and St. Mary's Whitechapel can be traced half a dozen of the Pilgrims. So there must have been many opportunities for Brewster to find a quiet refuge in the neighborhood, and he may have commuted between Nottinghamshire and the East End of London during the months when we have no definite knowledge of his whereabouts—we being in the same predicament as King James's pursuing agents. We do know that Bradford, having disposed of his house in Leyden in April 1619, was in the London area in the spring of 1620. The region retained its Non-Conformist atmosphere after the departure of the Pilgrims, being referred to in 1632 by the Bishop of London as a nest of Non-Comformists.

There is one other interesting clue, suggesting that Brewster may have had a son, Edward, an apprentice of the Stationers' Company in London, learning the printing trade and becoming a freeman in 1615. There is here (Banks, pp. 38–39) "a combination of surname, occupation and place identical with the Elder's life at that time," which is startling, if accidental. This Edward Brewster published between 1616 and 1640 twenty-five books, all sermons or theological controversy. One other clue supports the speculation of close relationship. Sir Robert Naunton wrote to Carleton at The Hague, August 1, 1619, "Brewster is frightened back into the Low Countries." Two days later he wrote, "Brewster's sonne, of his father's sect within this halfe year, now comes to Churche" and he adds that he had recovered a note from him (Brewster) to his son and had "committed the deliverer close until he discover where his father is." The pronouns are rather confusing. But nothing came of it. There may have been a son Edward or young Brewster relative of that name. To support the speculation, the records of the Virginia Company show that William Brewster and his son Edward bought shares in that enterprise in 1609. (Of course there may have been another William Brewster in the North.) In 1609 our William Brewster was already in Holland and scarcely well enough off to be purchasing shares in the Virginia Company. So far as we know, Jonathan was the eldest Brewster son and he was only about sixteen in 1609. If there was a son in London in 1619–20 he certainly wasn't hiding his father, or Sir Robert Naunton would have found him.

Wherever Brewster was during the last months of preparation for the voyage, and the probabilities favor London, he must have been accessible to his friends for consultation. What one would not give for a reliable clue! A garret with a hidden entrance door, for instance, like Anne Frank's hiding-place in Nazi-occupied Amsterdam; or a Priest's Hole in some country-house built into the chimney during the persecution of Catholics under Elizabeth; or just a house in the East End of London with two entrances on dark little lanes, as in Brewster's Leyden house. There must have been plenty of Stink Alleys in Aldgate and Houndsditch. Meanwhile his wife Mary and two young sons, Wrestling and Love, were probably in Leyden with Jonathan, who had married and had a house of his own. Two daughters, Fear and Patience, and Jonathan came to Plymouth on later boats. But Mary Brewster, William's wife, Wrestling and Love were all on the *Mayflower*, and were probably with the group from Leyden who finally set sail from Delfthaven for Southampton.

Reading Bradford's account of the protracted negotiations with the London Virginia Company and then with the Plymouth Virginia Company, after Cushman and Carver had obtained the Royal assent to embark on the expedition, makes one marvel that they really did at last succeed in sailing. And the Dutch had put in their oar, suggesting that the Leyden Church should emigrate to their colony on the Hudson River. It was finally settled that the group of London merchants would furnish financial support. Mr. Jessup writes that the agreement with the Merchant Adventurers for a seven-years' partnership makes Jacob's years of service to Laban for Rachel look by comparison like a handsome bargain. "These terms were regarded by those at Leyden as more fit for bond-slaves than honest men. . . . Every day's labor was to go into the common pool. . . . At the end of seven years, houses, land, and goods should be equally divided between settlers and merchants."

But finally the time came when the brethren in Leyden must depart. "They were accompanied," writes Bradford, "by most of their brethren out of the city to a town several miles off, called Delfthaven, where the ship lay ready to take them. So they left that good and pleasant city, which had been their resting place for nearly twelve years; but they knew they were pilgrims, and lifted up their eyes to the heavens, their dearest country, and quieted their spirits." Friends came from Leyden and Amsterdam to see them off, and there was much friendly entertainment and Christian discourse the night before they sailed. And the next day there were sighs and prayers and pithy speeches. "But the tide which stays for no man called them away . . . and their reverent pastor, falling down on his knees, and all with him, with watery cheeks commended them with most fervent prayers to the Lord and His blessing." With a favoring wind they came to Southampton, July 22, 1620, where the bigger ship from London was awaiting them, with the rest of the company. Was Brewster on hand, too, disguised?

Bradford's "they knew they were pilgrims" is a reference to the *Epistle to the Hebrews*, chapter 2, verse 13: "These all died in faith, not having received the promises, but having seen them afar off, and were persuaded of them and embraced them, and confessed that they were strangers and pilgrims on the earth. For they that say such things declare plainly that they seek a country." Here is the origin of "Pilgrim Fathers," used first, according to Mr. Jessup, by the Reverend Chandler Robbins in a memorial sermon preached in New Plymouth in 1793. Before that time the pilgrims were referred to as First-Comers and Fore-fathers. From this use in the sermon, Pilgrim Fathers came gradually into general acceptance.

Arrived at Southampton, after mutual congratulations with those who had gathered there, they had difficult business affairs to be straightened out with the agents of the Merchant Adventurers. Master Weston came down from London, became offended, and returned to London in displeasure. "They lacked," Bradford writes, "about £100 to clear their obligations; but he would not disburse a penny, and left them to shift as they could." Quoting from the letter they wrote to the "Merchants and Adventurers," "We are in such straits at present that we are forced to sell £60 worth of our provisions to clear the Haven, and put ourselves upon bare necessities, scarcely having any butter, no oil, not a soul to mend a shoe, nor every man a sword to his side, lacking many muskets, much armor, etc. . . . Thus saluting you all in love, we take our leave and rest."

The story of their troubles before the *Mayflower* finally left Plymouth September 6, 1620, includes the leak developed by the *Speedwell*, repaired at Dartmouth; then putting to sea again, discovering more leaks after they had sailed one hundred leagues from Land's End, both ships then turning back to Plymouth; the transfer of some passengers and provisions from the *Speedwell* to the *Mayflower*, others returning to London—especially those thought to be the least useful, because of their own weaknesses or the care of young children, and others because of their own fears. "And thus, like Gideon's army, this small number was divided." Bradford voices some reasonable suspicions about these leaks and the motives of the shipmaster of the *Speedwell* and his company, who were hired to spend a year in the colony and, losing heart at the prospect, plotted the stratagem to get out of their commitment— "by some of them confessed."

With all this coming and going and putting to sea and turning back to port and dividing up the passengers, one wonders how secret William Brewster's identity had become. Perhaps the King's pursuit agents had given up the chase and "connived" at the departure of the wanted man, as twelve years earlier in the North the magistrates let the Scrooby fugitives slip off to Holland. There must have been some danger of an informer, for though he was among friends in his congregation, the captain and crew and some of the passengers were outsiders. Some day, in an old trunk in the attic of an English country house, a letter or other document may accidentally turn up that will throw light on these last weeks spent in England by Elder Brewster. Stranger things than that have happened. And one of these accidental discoveries in recent years has revealed the story of four children, listed among the eighteen "family servants and young cousins" on the *Mayflower*. Their name was More—Jasper, Richard, Ellen, and an unnamed brother, from Shipton, Shropshire. Richard and the nameless brother are assigned to the "household of William Brewster," Jasper to John Carver's and Ellen to Edward Winslow's.

IX

Four Mayflower *Children*

Colonel Banks, author of *English Ancestry and Homes of the Pilgrim Fathers* (1929), suggested that the More children might have been pauper children in a London parish, whom the authorities turned over to Thomas Weston for settlement in the New World colony. "This seemed possible because 100 children were in fact handed over to the Virginia Company for transport and settlement by the Mayor and Aldermen of London in 1618, and 100 more in 1619." That seemed plausible enough from what was known in 1929. The whole story was finally disentangled from scattered facts and speculations and set forth in an article, *Children in the Mayflower*, by Anthony R. Wagner, published in the *Times* of London, June 29, 1959.

The article goes back to 1899 when the parish register of Shipton, Shropshire, was printed and a copy came to the notice of an American genealogist, Edwin A. Hill, who found three baptismal entries: Ellinora Moore, filia Samuelis More de Larden, May 24, 1612; Jasperus Moore, filius Samuelis Moore de Larden Generosi, August 8, 1613; and Richardus Moore, filius Samuelis Moore de Larden et uxoris ejus, November 13, 1614. Another document exists, a deposition made in New England on September 27, 1684, by "Richard Moore Senior aged seaventy yeares or thereabouts . . . that being in London at the House of Mr. Thomas Weston, Ironmonger in the year 1620, he was from thence transported to New Plymouth in New England." In 1684 Richardus Moore, born in 1614, would have been seventy years old. In 1620 when the *Mayflower* sailed he would have been a little less than six years old.

But this identification raised some puzzling questions. The Mores of Larden and Linley are an old landed family of Shropshire. How did four young children of such a family come to be in the charge of Thomas Weston in London, to be parcelled out among three Pilgrim households? Samuel More, registered as the father of Ellinora, Jasperus and Richardus, was born in 1594, and in 1610, at the early age of sixteen was married at Shipton to his third cousin, Catherine More, daughter and heiress of Jasper More of Larden. She was twenty-three. It is reasonable to suppose that this was a marriage of convenience, to keep property in the family. Then, surprisingly, we find Samuel More marrying a second wife in 1627, by whom he had seven children—the

eldest another Richard who in 1662 inherited the property at Linley and at Larden. Samuel More had a career
as a commander on the Parliament side in the Civil War,
and he has his place in the *Dictionary of National Biography*. Where were the children of his first marriage?

Dr. Hill, in the absence of any explanation, impro-
vised one: perhaps, left a widower with young children
at the presumed death of Catherine, and being a man of
Puritan sympathies, Samuel More might have sought
"a safe asylum for his helpless motherless children in the
new commonwealth about to be founded beyond the
seas by men of his own religious and political faith."
"To others," comments the author of the *Times* article
from which we are quoting, "such treatment might seem
more to resemble that of the Babes in the Wood." The
truth turned out to be more credible and much more
scandalous. Mr. Wagner asked his friend, Mr. Jasper
More of Linley, about this family puzzle, and Mr. More
searched the family archives, during the winter "when
snow kept him indoors." How satisfying to have family
archives for a winter's day! Mr. More came upon a
document that solved the problem. It was the draft of a
declaration addressed by Samuel More to Sir James
Ley, Lord Chief Justice of England, replying to a petition made to the Lord Chief Justice by Samuel More's
wife Catherine. The declaration states that by 1616
Samuel had become aware of "the common fame of the
adulterous life of the said Catherine More with one
Jacob Blakeway, a fellow of mean parentage and condi-

tion, which continued long before the said Samuel suspected it, and after it was known to the said Samuel the apparent likeness and resemblance of most of the said children in their visages and lineaments of their bodies to the said Blakeway" made him want to disclaim them. Catherine and Blakeway continued to meet together, Catherine—who seems to have been able to hold her own—justifying her acts by alleging a pre-contract with Blakeway before her marriage to Samuel, which made him her husband in the sight of God. She could not sufficiently prove this by witnesses, "yet it was all one before God, as she said."

Samuel took action that seems justified, but of course we do not know Catherine's side of the story. It took until 1620 for this pair to be divorced. The first thing More did was to cut off the entail, thus disinheriting the children. But he took care to have them maintained and educated in the country, with certain tenants of his father's and also in the town—"presumably at Linley or More." But Catherine proved troublesome: "Unto which children the said Catherine often repaired and there used divers exclamations and slanders and did tear their clothes from their backs, by reason of which and other her continued lewd demeanour the said Samuel's parents were continually vexed and grieved, they forbearing to take the children into their house to avoid her slanders (if it should have pleased God to visit any of them with death) of being murderers of them: and withal to shun the continual sight of their great grief of such a spurious brood." One cannot have much sympathy for Samuel's parents, who must have arranged this marriage of a 16-year-old son with a 23-year-old woman.

It was Catherine who sought in the ecclesiastical court a divorce and license to remarry, "while Blakeway obtained a pardon for the adultery with her which he admitted." There must have been extenuating circumstances, if he obtained a pardon, especially as he was a man "of mean condition." There is probably more to this story than the documents reveal. In 1618 "Samuel brought a successful action against Blakeway for trespass and damage on Samuel's property at Larden." And finally in 1619, "sentence of divorce between Samuel and Catherine was given in the Court of Audience and a year later was confirmed on appeal by the Court of Delegates." Who appealed, one wonders? The legal intricacies leave quite a bit of the story tangled up.

But what happened to the little Babes in the Wood? In July, 1620, by Samuel's direction the four children were brought up to London by a servant of Samuel's father and delivered to Philemon Powell, who was to turn them over to John Carver and Robert Cushman. These in turn received them and "did covenant and agree to transport them into Virginia and to see that they should be sufficiently kept and maintained with meat, drink, apparel, lodging and other necessaries and that at the end of seven years they should have 50 acres of land apiece in the country of Virginia, for performance whereof they entered into articles and they, together with one Mr. Weston, an honest and sufficient merchant, gave bond to Mr. Paul Harris, cousin german of the said Samuel, in the sum of £120." Samuel paid through his cousin £80 and also £20 more in adventure from the profits of which the children's portion might be increased. When Samuel made his will in 1655, "he made no mention at all of his first wife or her children." He probably did not know that—as Bradford tells us—the little girl Ellen died soon after the ship's arrival at New Plymouth, and both Jasper and the unnamed brother died in the epidemic of the first winter. Richard survived, presumably brought up in the Brewster household, dying many years later in 1698 or 1699 at Salem, where his gravestone in Charter Street Cemetery still exists, the only one surviving of any *Mayflower* passenger. He married and left several children and "from his daughter Susanna, the wife of Captain Samuel Dutch, many New England families can show descent."

Brewster must have known the whole story when he took two little discarded boys into his family. Richardus More was lucky to find such a haven.

X

Of Their Voyage and Safe Arrival at Cape Cod

The tale of the voyage with all its trials and hardships, based on Bradford's account, has been often retold. After he has described the landing, he turns back a little to record an event of historical significance: the signing before they came ashore of the *Mayflower* Compact. A troublesome situation had arisen because the place where the ship had dropped anchor was not where they were supposed to be; they had no legal right to establish a plantation there. An unauthorized landing held out interesting possibilities to some mutinous and discontented spirits aboard among the "strangers" who had been recruited by the London Merchants. These strangers, as Bradford puts it, had let fall speeches: "That when they got ashore they would use their liberty; that none had power to command them, the patent procured being for Virginia, and not for New England, which belonged to another company, with which the Virginia Company had nothing to do." Mr. Jessup sums it up neatly: "The Pilgrim leaders were well accustomed to dealing with difficult people and met these mutinous mutterings with a masterly stroke of diplomacy. They called the menfolk into the cabin of the *Mayflower* and presented them with the famous compact, which became the foundation document for the government of the colony. Its immediate effect on the quarrelsome was all that could be desired by its designers, and for posterity the first American State Paper was signed, sealed and delivered." There are forty-one signatures, leading off with Carver, Bradford, Winslow, Brewster, Allerton, Standish, and Alden. The date—November 11, 1620. The loyal subjects of King James covenant and combine together into a civil body politic, for their better ordering and preservation and furthering the ends stated—the advancement of the Christian faith and the honor of king and country. By virtue of the pact, they would enact just and equal laws, ordinances, and offices from time to time for the general good of the colony, to which they promise due submission and obedience.

"Thus," writes Henry Steele Commager in *Living Ideas in America*, "at the very beginning of our history, the settlers were confronted with the problem of liberty versus order. They solved that problem in what was to be a characteristic fashion. Taking for granted that authority was inherent in them, the Pilgrim leaders drew up the *Mayflower* Compact—an extension to civil conditions of the customary church covenant and of the sea covenant. As the Plymouth settlers were never able to get a charter, the *Mayflower* Compact remained the only constitution of the colony." The first civic appointment was that of John Carver to be governor for a year. After he died in 1621, Bradford was elected and re-elected for thirty years.

The life in the New World of Elder Brewster and his family was the life of the Plymouth Colony. How he lived it and fulfilled his duties as Elder is sufficiently summed up in his friend Bradford's words after his death. Like his father, he died intestate. His two surviving sons were Jonathan and Love. Four old friends took charge of settling the estate; one of them, Thomas Prence, was the husband of Patience Brewster. The others were Bradford, Winslow, and Standish. The inventory—printed in Volume 3 of *The Mayflower Descendant*, 1901—appraises the estate at £150. To the items of clothing mentioned earlier, add a "pistoll," a rapier, a silver beaker and spoon, a tobacco case. There was a house and farm at Duxbury, where Love and his family lived; and among the items listed are an old cow, a red cow, a yoke of oxen ten years old, and "half a young Sowe"—the last inviting speculation. Was it dried or smoked or pickled or just destined to that fate?

But it is the library of over 400 volumes that tells us most about the Elder's range of interest. Compared with that of Governor Bradford—80 volumes—it is impressive. It includes both Latin and English books: among them Bacon's *Advancement of Learning*, Machiavelli's *Princeps*, Camden's *"Brittain"*; works by Hakluyt, Raleigh, Dekker, Erasmus; and, to be expected, theological treatises mentioned earlier in connection with his Cambridge residence, and works by Luther, Calvin, Peter the Martyr, Beza, and others. There is a copy of *The Perth Assembly*, which proved the undoing of the Pilgrim Press. And there are books on silkworms and on medicine. A rather surprising item is *The Tragedy of Messalina, the Roman Emperesse, as acted by the Companie of Her Majestie's Revels*, London, 1640. More in line with religion is *The Psalms of David in metre . . . to be sung and plaide upon the Lute, the Orpharyon, Citterne, or Base Violl.* London, 1599. By Richard Alison—an important composer of the Elizabethan period.

George F. Willison, in his introduction to the modern English version of Bradford's *Plymouth Colony* for the Classics Club edition, calls Elder Brewster "the most lovable of all the Plymouth 'Saincts.'" One hopes that when the Elder was neither exercising his "singular good gift of Prayer," or moving and stirring the affections by his preaching, or busy with his church duties of suppressing errors and contentions in the congregation, or just being "very sociable and pleasant among his friends," he may have had hours to spend among his books. There is no portrait of him; the only surviving portrait of any one of the Pilgrims is that of Edward Winslow. But one can fancy him in his study, wearing perhaps that violet cloth coat, the doublet, the black silk stockings, with a quilted cap on his head as protection against winter drafts,—reading *Cartwright against Whitgift* and recalling Cambridge controversies, or Machiavelli's *Prince* and remembering his years with Sir William Davison in that far-off England of Elizabeth and Mary Queen of Scots.

Selected Bibliography

Arber, Edward: *The Story of the Pilgrim Fathers 1606–1623*. London, 1897.

Banks, Charles Edward: *The English Ancestry and Homes of the Pilgrim Fathers, who came to Plymouth on the Mayflower in 1620, the Fortune in 1621, and the Anne and the Little James in 1623*. New York, The Grafton Press, 1929.

Bartlett, Rev. W. H.: *The Pilgrim Fathers, or The Founders of New England in the Reign of James the First*. London, 1853.

Bowman, G. E.: *Mayflower Descendant*, 11 (1900) and 111 (1901), "Elder William Brewster's Inventory," pp. 15–31.

Bradford, William: *The History of Plymouth Colony. A Modern English Version, with an introduction by George F. Willison*. Published for the Classics Club. Walter J. Black, New York, 1948.

——— *Of Plymouth Plantation, The Pilgrims in America.* Edited with an Introduction by Harvey Wish. New York, Capricorn Books, 1962.

Burgess, Walter H.: *John Robinson, Pastor of the Pilgrim Fathers. A Study of his Life and Times.* London, Williams & Norgate, 1920, New York, Harcourt, Brace & Howe, 1920.

Dexter, Henry Martyn and Morton Dexter: *The England and Holland of the Pilgrims.* Boston, Houghton & Mifflin, 1905.

Gill, Crispin: *Mayflower Remembered, A History of the Plymouth Pilgrims.* Newton Abbot, Devon, David & Charles, 1970. (Illustrated with photographs, maps, and drawings, of Southampton, Dartmouth, Plymouth, Leyden, Scrooby, etc. The author has written in interesting detail of Plymouth, Devon, which had been "playing its part in North American history for half a century and more before the *Mayflower* made her chance call at the English port.")

Harris, James Rendel and Jones, Stephen K.: *The Pilgrim Press:* Bibliographical & Historical Memorial of the books printed at Leyden by the Pilgrim Fathers [that is, by William Brewster and his associates, with a chapter on the location of the Pilgrim Press in Leyden, by Dr. Plooji]. Cambridge (Eng.), Heffer, 1922. Note: Contains photograph of Brewster's Printing House as it was in 1922, and maps showing position of the house.

Holloway, Naomi D.: *The Genealogy of Mary Wentworth, who became the wife of William Brewster.* (Copies may be purchased from Mrs. Perle Lee Holloway, 1305 5th Street, Boulder, Colorado, 80302.) 1969 (?)

Hunter, Joseph: *Collections concerning the Church or Con-*

gregation of Protestant Separatists formed at Scrooby. London, 1854.

—— *Collections concerning the Early History of the Founders of New Plymouth.* London, 1849.

Jessup, Edmund F. (Rector of Babworth, England): *The Mayflower Story.* Retford, England, 1962.

Langdon, George D., Jr.: *Pilgrim Colony, 1620–1691.* New Haven, Yale University Press, 1969.

MacGibbon, Jean: *A Special Providence, The Story of the Children in the Mayflower.* London, Hamish Hamilton, 1964. Illustrated by William Stobbs. (A book for children, the story is supposed to be told by Giles Hopkinson, one of the children who came over in the *Mayflower;* vividly dramatized on the basis of the known facts. Scenes at the London docks, and at Southampton and Plymouth. The author's speculation (not documented, but plausible) is that Elder Brewster, hiding out in Scrooby, made his way across country to the Hopkinson home in Gloucestershire, where he was safe till he could be smuggled to the coast. There at night a small boat picked him up, along with bags of nails destined for the *Mayflower,* at a small inlet, and eluding guards, rowed down to Southampton Water, where the *Speedwell,* just arrived from Holland, and the *Mayflower* were both anchored. The young narrator is made to reflect that if he and the two men who managed this rescue had missed the tide and had been captured, it would not have mattered much. "But it would have mattered to all our people if they had lost William Brewster.")

McGinn, Donald J.: *John Penry and the Marprelate Controversy.* New Brunswick, N.J., Rutgers University Press, 1966.

Massachusetts Historical Society, Proceedings, Series 12,

Vol. 5, pp. 37–85, 1890. (A catalogue of Elder Brewster's library compiled by William Bradford, Thomas Prence, and John Reyner, communicated by Henry M. Dexter.)
Pierce, William: *John Penry: His Life, Times and Writings.* London, Hodder & Stoughton, 1923.
Sitwell, Dame Edith: *The Queens and the Hive.* Boston, Atlantic Monthly Press, 1962.
Steele, Ashbel: *Chief of the Pilgrims, or the Life and Time of William Brewster.* Philadelphia, J. B. Lippincott & Co., 1857.
Usher, Roland G.: *The Pilgrims and Their History.* New York, Macmillan, 1918.
Walker, Thomas Alfred: *Peterhouse.* [Plates, including a portrait.] Cambridge (Eng.), Heffer, 1935.
Willison, George: *Saints and Strangers.* London, Wm. Heineman, Ltd., 1946.

Natural History, Journal of the American Museum of Natural History, vol. LXXVIII, No. 9, November, 1969. "The Reality of the Pilgrim Fathers," by James Deetz. This article describes how the little community of Plymouth, Massachusetts, has been recreated in full scale, two miles south of its original site, as it looked to the Dutch trader Isaac de Rasieres in 1627. It is being recreated as an outdoor museum by Plimouth Plantation, a non-profit educational organization, founded twenty years ago to create an understanding of the Pilgrims and seventeenth century America through exhibits, publications, films, and educational programs. The recreated village seeks to communicate an understanding of the way of life in Plymouth during the colony's first ten years. During these years, William Brewster was the Elder of the congregation and Bradford the Governor.

In 1627, the Elder's wife, Mary Wentworth, died. The article describes how the village is presented as a living community, where people perform the routine tasks of that time. A visit to this fascinating recreated village would help us to imagine what it was like to live there with Elder Brewster in 1627.

The Mayflower Quarterly, published by the General Society of *Mayflower* Descendants, in the November, 1968 issue, has a note about the activities of the Elder William Brewster Society, which was organized at Plymouth, Mass., in September, 1963 by Brewster descendants. In 1968 the Society erected a cenotaph in memory of Elder Brewster and his wife on Burial Hill in Plymouth.

A plaque on the Post Office in Plymouth, Mass., reads:

> Site of one of the Houses built in 1621. This lot was assigned to William Brewster, Elder of the Colony, and Spiritual Leader until 1629, when the first Minister was engaged.

A notice on the drinking fountain in front of the Post Office states that the water issuing from the fountain is piped from the William Brewster spring. A pleasant little stream flows through a park, once a slum area, now "The Brewster Gardens."

In connection with the "*Mayflower* 1970" celebrations in England to commemorate the 350th anniversary of the sailing of the *Mayflower*, the Council of the London Borough of Southwark published *The Mayflower and Pilgrim Story: Chapters from Rotherhithe and Southwark*.

This little booklet of 55 pages is illustrated by drawings from prints and photographs in the Southwark Collection. It was produced by members of the staff of the London

Borough of Southwark Libraries Department. There is a bibliography. Rotherhithe, two miles down the river from Old London Bridge, was the home of Captain Christopher Jones of the *Mayflower*. He returned there the year after the voyage, and his grave is in the churchyard of St. Mary's, Rotherhithe. From Rotherhithe the *Mayflower* must have set sail to join the *Speedwell* at Southampton. In Great Dover Street in Southwark is the Pilgrim Fathers Memorial Church, claiming descent from persecuted dissenters who met secretly at Southwark during the late 16th and early 17th centuries, some of whom suffered martyrdom. "It is the claim of the present church that some of those who sailed in the *Mayflower* were associated with this ancient church." (Quote from *The Mayflower and Pilgrim Story*.)

The Southwark Collection, from which the illustrations are taken, is in the Newington District Library, Walworth Road, London, S.E.17.

Index